...anagement

D1386948

ABOUT THE AUTHOR

Michael Regester is a leading international adviser on crisis management, helping companies to anticipate and deal with all forms of corporate crisis. He is a Director and Head of the Crisis Management division of London-based Charles Barker Traverse-Healy Limited, part of the Charles Barker Group plc, one of the UK's foremost communications consultancies, and is professionally regarded as 'in the big league' of crisis management.

He has pioneered the development and implementation of crisis prevention and crisis communications programmes for organisations, following his own experience in handling Gulf Oil's Bantry Bay disaster in 1979 — one of the worst disasters in the history of the oil industry.

The author of many articles on crisis management, Michael Regester also lectures on the subject throughout the world. He is married with two daughters and lives in Cambridge.

Crisis Management

What to do when the Unthinkable Happens

by

Michael Regester

Department for Work & Pensions
Information Services

533946

Location:	Date:
ADI	19·03 12
Class:	
	658. 405 CRi

Business Books

WIT

Copyright © Michael Regester 1989

First published in Great Britain by
Business Books Limited
An imprint of Century Hutchinson Limited
62-65 Chandos Place, London, WC2N 4NW

Century Hutchinson Australia (Pty) Limited
89-91 Albion Street, Surry Hills,
New South Wales 2010, Australia

Century Hutchinson New Zealand Limited
P O Box 40-086, 32-34 View Road, Glenfield,
Auckland 10, New Zealand

Century Hutchinson South Africa (Pty) Limited
P O Box 337, Bergvlei 2012, South Africa

British Library Cataloguing in Publication Data

Regester, Michael
    Crisis management: how to turn a
    crisis into an opportunity.
    1. Crisis management
    I. Title
    658.4   HD49

    ISBN 0-09-173954-3

Printed and bound in Great Britain by
Courier International Ltd, Tiptree, Essex

Contents

Acknowledgements

My grateful appreciation to Katie Arber for the research; to Nicci Griffiths, Anne Carby and Jenny Mitchell for typing the manuscript; to all those who provided valuable advice in compiling this book; and especially to my wife Christine for her support and encouragement.

Preface

If you currently hold, or expect to hold, a position in your organization in which you would have responsibility for dealing with a major crisis, this book is intended for you. You may have already risen to the dizzy heights of chief executive. You may be a finance director, personnel director, plant manager, safety officer, corporate lawyer or public relations manager. You may be entirely at ease in implementing your day-to-day tasks against which your performance and results are judged. Perhaps the one area in which you are most vulnerable is if the totally unexpected happened? Could you cope? Have you the people around you who could cope? Do you have plans, procedures and equipment in place to help you deal with the situation? Only you know the answers.

Revealingly, a survey of chief executives in the United States conducted in 1985 by Stephen B Fink, president of Lexicon Communications, found that 89 per cent believed 'a crisis in business as inevitable as death and taxes'. Only 50 per cent admitted they had a plan for managing one. Into which half would you fit?

This concise book is intended as a practical guide for executives who might one day have to deal with the unexpected. It argues the case for planning, preparation and training. It examines some well-documented case histories of corporate disasters and assesses the lessons to be drawn from each. It attempts to formulate some practical guidelines for you to consider adapting and putting into place within your own organization. These are distilled from a compendium of advice and experience from experts who have made a study of, or have been faced with, major corporate crises.

PREFACE

This book alone will not equip you to deal with corporate crisis, but it should alert you to the danger signals, set you thinking about your own organization's ability to deal with a crisis, and provide you with a crisis management structure for adaptation to your own particular requirements.

CHAPTER 1

Tales of the Unexpected

To set the scene, this first chapter looks at some different crises which have affected various organizations; and, with the fortunate benefit of hindsight, develops a list of basic ingredients which need to be considered when approaching the management of crisis.

In recent times, the disasters at Chernobyl and Bhopal have served notice on governments and companies alike of the need to be prepared to cope with crisis; to communicate effectively about what has happened and the steps being taken to remedy the situation. Failure to do so may one day cause governments to fall and has already caused companies to close. Regrettably, the prospects for companies having to face some form of major crisis, more than once, are greater than ever before. Human error, lack of judgement, lack of anticipation, corporate greed, mechanical failure — all combine to guarantee that a major crisis will present itself to company executives sooner or later. Nor does a crisis have to be on a large scale to be dangerous: a small fire in the computer room may cripple a medium-sized company.

And why should this be so unexpected? After all, much of mankind's progress has come from learning by mistakes. In some fields, for example at the leading edge of technology, companies must expect to square up to more than most. That is what the failure of the US Challenger mission in 1986 was all about — learning tragically and too late, from a whole series of mistakes. But one of the most dangerous aspects of modern crisis management is that corporate crisis is so much more visible than it used to be. Evolution in the media has led to the increased importance of something called 'accountability'. A few years ago a company was accountable for its actions to its shareholders and, perhaps, to its employees. Today, little that a company does escapes outside scrutiny. Companies have rapidly been made accountable not simply to shareholders and employees but to politicians, local authorities, environmental pressure groups, the media, local community groups, bankers, brokers, financial analysts and a host of other 'interested' parties.

An increased public expectation of corporate accountability means that when the unexpected occurs a variety of influential outside audiences want fast, accurate explanations of what has happened and details of what is being done to remedy the situation.

Most crises happen bewilderingly quickly. News of what has gone wrong spreads with equal speed. Companies not equipped to cope with a crisis face a number of unpleasant perils, which can include boycotts of company products, a dramatic fall in share price, major lawsuits, threats of bankruptcy, reduced credit ratings, immeasurable damage to the company's reputation, demands for resignations by company executives, and even possible closure of part or all of the company.

Companies in crisis will have to face some of these consequences, in any case. It is their ability to deal with the crisis that will pull them through and, possibly, gain them friends along the way. How is this possible?

The Tylenol tale

Never in corporate history has an organization in crisis gained as much public and editorial sympathy as Johnson & Johnson did in the US for their conduct throughout the Tylenol-related poisonings and their aftermath. The day before cyanide-laced Tylenol tablets caused deaths in the Chicago area on 29 and 30 September 1982, Tylenol commanded 35 per cent of the US adult over-the-counter analgesic market, accounted for some $450 million of annual sales and contributed over 15 per cent of Johnson & Johnson's overall profits. At first, just three deaths from cyanide poisoning were associated with the capsules. As the news spread as many as 250 deaths and illnesses in various parts of the US were suspected as being part of a widespread pattern. Eventually enquiries from the media alone were logged at over 2,500.

After testing eight million tablets, Johnson & Johnson found that no more than 75, all from one batch, were contaminated. The final death toll was seven, all in the Chicago area, but the alarm had been spread nationwide. Surveys showed later that 94 per cent of consumers were aware that Tylenol were associated with the poisonings.

Johnson & Johnson later went on to relaunch the product and to win the *Silver Anvil Award* of the Public Relations Society of America for its handling of the crisis. Within five months of the disaster, the company had recovered 70 per cent of its one-third share of this huge market. The company had clearly positioned itself as a champion of the consumer, given meaning to the concept of corporate social responsibility, and demonstrated communication expertise that will be hard to equal for years to come. *How?*

Key to the success of the way in which the Tylenol case was handled lay in the assumption of the '*worst possible scenario*'. Ironically, the closest thing the company had to a crisis plan was its credo that its first concern must be for the public and its customers. Its credo served it well.

To its credit, Johnson & Johnson lost little time in recalling millions of bottles of its extra-strength Tylenol capsules, while it reportedly spent half a million dollars warning physicians, hospitals and distributors of the possible dangers. At the time, the *Wall Street Journal* wrote: 'The company chose to take a large loss rather than expose anyone to further risk. The "anti-corporation movement" may have trouble squaring that with the devil theories it purveys.' Additionally, at a time when the US government and local authorities in Chicago and elsewhere were pushing for new drug safety laws, Johnson & Johnson saw a marketing opportunity — and took it — by edging out its competitors in the $1.2 billion analgesic category, it was the first in the industry, after the recall, to respond to the 'national mandate' for tamper-resistant packaging and the new regulations imposed by the US Food and Drug Administration.

When Johnson & Johnson promptly recalled Tylenol capsules from the market the company demonstrated its concern for consumers' health — as one might reasonably have expected it to. It would have been a great mistake to try to pretend that nothing was wrong (as Firestone Tyre and Rubber Company officials did when Firestone 500 tyres started disintegrating).

The plaudits which Johnson & Johnson received, leading to, most importantly, market share recovery, stemmed from its decision to adopt a worst-scenario stance when it might easily have restricted the recall simply to the Chicago area and saved itself millions of dollars. Had it done so then its Tylenol sales would almost certainly have suffered more dramatic losses because of poison-tampering hysteria — losses that would have been far more difficult to recover because of continued uncertainty and loss of public trust.

Dr Leonard Snyder, Managing Director of the 2nd Opinion Company, has pointed out: 'The total recall was a prudent marketing decision. The marketing perspective which prevails today views profits as an ancillary of consumer benefit, whereas under yesterday's concept of marketing, profits are considered a function of sales. Unfortunately too many companies, both national and multinational, still predicate their marketing strategies as sales and profits activities.'

More to the point, however, are the lessons which can be drawn from this brief outline of the Tylenol case to help us start to formulate an approach to crisis management.

1 *Faced with disaster, consider the worst possible scenario — and act accordingly.* After all, if the magnitude of the crisis turns out to require less than the actions you have taken, you cannot be criticized for being over-cautious. You may even gain praise and sympathy for your actions. On the other hand, if your response turns out to be below what was needed to deal with the situation, you will be condemned as uncaring, insensitive, unintelligent and money-grabbing.

2 *When the dust has settled, look to see what lessons you might be able to teach the rest of industry from your experience — and act accordingly.* In other words, look for some initiatives which you may be able to seize. First and foremost, you will be acting in a responsible manner, and seen to be, but your initiative may also lead to competitive advantage.

3 *Have a crisis management plan.* Johnson & Johnson had a credo; the company also acted intelligently. Assume your own worst scenario — that you won't know what to do unless you've thought about it, written it down, and tested it. More about that later.

Never forget that company reputations are hard won through many years of careful policy-making and a heavy investment in communications programmes. A major crisis, perceived mismanagement of the aftermath, and a failure to communicate effectively during and after the crisis can destroy that reputation in a matter of days, even hours.

The Bhopal tragedy

The accident at Bhopal is an extreme example of a crisis. The sheer magnitude and horror of the tragedy stunned the world. Nevertheless, the problems Union Carbide had to deal with afterwards were broadly the same set of problems presented to any organization staring corporate crisis in the face. It was the scale of human suffering which set it apart.

Shortly after midnight on 3 December 1984, poison gas seeped from an underground storage tank and formed a deadly white cloud over an area of twenty-five square miles. By morning the leaking gas had killed more than 1,200 people, and some 20,000 others had been injured. Most of those who died had been sleeping. They suffocated as the gas attacked their lungs and blood. The gas, methyl isocyanate, was the principal ingredient for pesticides used by Indian farmers and fruit growers. The pesticides were produced in a factory owned by the Indian subsidiary of the Union Carbide Corporation.

When it received word of the disaster at corporate headquarters in Danburg, Connecticut, the company called an immediate worldwide halt to production and shipment of methyl isocyanate and despatched a doctor and four technicians to India to discover the causes of the leak. The next day, risking certain arrest, Warren M Anderson, Union Carbide's chairman, flew to Bhopal for a first-hand investigation. By Friday 7 December, over 2,000 Bhopal residents had died. More than 20,000 were sick or injured.

Meanwhile, members of the news media, representatives of environmental groups, politicians and so-called 'experts' on poisonous gases became involved. Stories about Bhopal hit the headlines, and prime-time news broadcasts about the disaster were on television and radio within hours and stayed there for more than a month.

Union Carbide officials were beseiged with questions,

the answers to which were largely unknown for several days. Nonetheless, the news gaps were filled by people who speculated on the causes of the disaster, on the design of the safety systems at Union Carbide's plant, on the advisability of working with deadly chemicals in heavily populated areas, on the likelihood of extensive damage claims against the company, and on corporate responsibility in general. Many of the resulting news stories were acknowledged to be unconfirmed reports. Nevertheless, they made headlines at the expense of Union Carbide.

But even in a fast-breaking crisis like Bhopal, it is possible to take early initiatives. Union Carbide did this on the day of the disaster by calling a press conference at a hotel in Connecticut. The conference room was jammed with reporters, and much of the questioning, naturally, was of a speculative nature. But it was all urgent because journalists were under enormous pressure to produce stories.

Union Carbide was able to tell them that they were sending help to India: medical supplies, respirators and a doctor with extensive knowledge of the effects of methyl isocyanate. Later, they announced that they were sending a team of technical experts to examine the plant and determine what went wrong.

Because of its magnitude, we will consider different aspects of the Bhopal disaster later in this book. At this stage, it may be worth commenting that history will probably judge Union Carbide by the size of settlement it provides victims of the disaster, and the speed with which it settles (matters by no means entirely in the company's hands). From what we've seen so far, however, we can already begin to add to our approach to crisis management.

4 *Be prepared to demonstrate human concern for what has happened.* Warren Anderson did by flying straight to the scene of the disaster. When faced with

a problem, companies all too often forget they are made up of groups of people. Have a figurehead available to express how the company is feeling about what has happened and what action it is taking to ease the situation.

5 *In communications terms, be prepared to seize early initiatives by rapidly establishing the company as the single authoritative source of information about what has gone wrong and what steps the organization is taking to remedy the situation.* Union Carbide managed this, at least in part, by staging an early press conference and undertaking a variety of other measures.

The need for effective communications during a time of crisis cannot be over emphasized. Often, a company's reputation will be judged as much by the way it communicates about the crisis as the cause of the crisis itself. Effective communications during a crisis can also play a vital role in containing the effects of the crisis itself.

Tales of financial panic

Let's look at a classic 'run on the bank', a financial panic. On 6 September 1982, queues began forming outside the Yuen Long branch of the Hang Lung Bank in Hong Kong. The next day a thousand people besieged the branch. Then the panic spread to the other branches. Some HK$60 million was withdrawn, about six times the usual amount.

There was nothing wrong with the Hang Lung but a rumour had spread that it was banker to a firm that had crashed with massive debts. (In fact, it was not banker to the firm in question and the company itself was perfectly sound and trading profitably.)

Everyone swung into action. Central bankers prepared to bail the bank out and the government expressed its confidence in the Hang Lung in an effort to get depositors to leave their money where it was. What stopped the run and restored confidence was a simple statement in the press. The Hang Lung had assembled a liquid reserve of HK$1 billion to cover the requirements of any depositor wishing to withdraw his cash. The effect was almost instant. The panic stopped.

6 *Whenever possible, look for ways of using the media as part of your armoury for containing the effects of the crisis.*

The president of Norwest Bank in Minneapolis was, so the story goes, carving his Thanksgiving turkey when a friend called: 'Jim, your bank is on fire!' Some hundred miles away, the Bank's vice president of corporate communications was visiting relatives and was startled to see a television report on a major fire in downtown Minneapolis.

What was to become the biggest blaze in Minneapolis' history also served as a baptism of fire for Norwest Bank's crisis contingency plans. Six months earlier, the company had updated its public relations plan whose main purpose was to assure customers that, in the event of an emergency, their funds were safe and business would continue as usual. The revised plan provided for the location of vital back-up records, telephone numbers of key executives to be notified, and the availability of office space should departments have to be relocated at short notice.

Even as the flames gutted the 16-storey structure, the PR plan was activated. The bank's president went on radio and TV advising depositors that accounts and valuables were safe, the building fully insured and that all other branches would open for business the following day.

With a staff of a dozen bank public relations people as well as personnel from two outside firms, the bank set up special telephone hotlines for customers, employees and the media from a 'war room' established in a building across the street. Personal letters were sent and phone calls made from appropriate departmental heads to allay any fears that assets were in danger. 'A lot of people are unsophisticated', observed the bank's vice president of corporate communications. 'They think if a bank burns, their money burns with it.' The press were given unlimited access to bank executives.

When Norwest reopened for business, bank representatives, easily identified by red and white T-shirts emblazoned 'NW Bank Info', were spotted throughout downtown Minneaplois directing customers to bank locations.

In all, the crisis programme cost Norwest about $400,000. Later, the bank's president remarked: 'The Thanksgiving Day fire was one of the most traumatic experiences of my life. But if you're going to have a catastrophe, this is the kind to have. There was no business lost, no hostile press, and nobody got hurt.' Panic had been averted.

In a sense, Norwest was lucky. But the bank deserves full credit for the fact that it had a crisis contingency plan. Not only did such a plan exist, but it had been recently revised and updated. The bank also demonstrated considerable creative initiative, for example, in using some of its representatives wearing, presumably pre-prepared, T-shirts to direct customers to other bank branches.

Norwest Bank got it right. The bank's president was not frightened to appear on TV and radio to reassure and advise customers; the bank set up telephone 'hotlines' for customers, employees and the media; and it established a 'war room' staffed by personnel whose role it was to manage the crisis. What new crisis management guidelines can be drawn from the Norwest experience?

7 *At the outset of a crisis, quickly establish a 'war room',
or Emergency Control Centre and staff it with senior
personnel trained to fulfill specific roles designed to
contain and manage the crisis.* At a time of crisis,
normal operations of the organization have to
continue so it is important that those designated to
man the 'war room' can be released from their normal
duties without jeopardizing the smooth running of
day-to-day activities. They will also need 'alternates'
in case they are away on vacation or sick; or in the
event of a long-running crisis which requires a
change of shift.

8 *Set up telephone hotlines to cope with the floods of
additional incoming calls that will be received during
a crisis.* If possible, install an emergency switchboard
(before the crisis starts) or have dedicated phone lines
whose numbers can be released to the media, and via
the media to others. Have personnel trained to man
the hotlines.

The sorry tale of the baby milk scandal

In the early 1970s there was growing disquiet about the
marketing and promotion of infant formula milk in
developing countries. There was some evidence linking
the indiscriminate sale of milk powder by western
multinational companies to infant malnutrition. The
press scented a story. The companies did not respond.

In 1977, the now famous 'Nestlé boycott' began in the
US. Members of the Infant Formula Action Coalition set
about trying to persuade American citizens not to buy
Nestlé products because of the Swiss company's activities
in developing countries. The company did not respond
adequately by telling its side of the story, so it got
pilloried by the press. The sorry tale of the baby milk
scandal dragged on and on — for ten years. American

journalists such as Milton Moskowitz saw the Nestlé boycott as: '. . . an intense battle, the fiercest and most emotional ever waged against a major multinational company.'

So much has been learnt from the Nestlé boycott by the international business community that it's worth taking a detailed look at Rafael D Pagan Jr's description of the sequence of events and the company's responses to its critics. (Rafael D Pagan Jr was President of the Nestlé Coordination Centre for Nutrition Inc, based in Washington, DC, USA.) He is chief executive of Pagan International.

It wasn't until January 1984, that the International Nestlé Boycott Committee (INBC), announced the suspension of the boycott in recognition of Nestlé's implementation of the World Health Organisation's Code of Marketing of Breastmilk Substitutes.

'Nestle has moved forward to become a model for the whole industry, a model that creates a new standard for corporate behaviour', said Douglas A Johnson, Chairman of the leading boycott group in the United States. The institution of the boycott, with the support of the socially concerned, posed fundamental questions not only for Nestlé but for the concept of multinational business enterprise as a legitimate and useful force in the world. Similarly, the end of the boycott demonstrated that profit-orientated businesses can be and often are responsive to social concerns. In retrospect, the boycott never should have taken place. It represented a major failure by a large multinational company to identify legitimate concerns early enough, compounded by inadequate communication to influential opinion leaders of the policy responses actually made by the company. Unfortunately, the company in particular, and the industry as a whole, did not counter adequately the allegations of activist critics. Moreover, the company's cold scientific and legal responses to the moral issues raised by some sincere religious leaders gave the impression of intransigence rather than the care and concern that was no doubt felt but which the company failed to communicate.

When the infant formula issue was first raised in 1970, Nestlé attempted to define it as a nutrition and health care issue. The company's scientific and statistical response offended the religious and people of conscience. They were further alienated by the slowness of some in Nestlé to recognize the legitimacy and sincerity of their concerns.

When a small Swiss activist group accused Nestlé of 'killing babies', Nestlé sued for libel and won. But a long, drawn-out, highly publicized trial turned the legal victory into a public relations disaster that led directly to the boycott. When the political activists called for the boycott, leaders of religious and socially concerned groups joined it. Some of them had come to believe, on the basis of the company's seeming indifference to the larger social and political issues, that profit-orientated enterprises were so concerned with making money that they condoned practices that harmed societies of people.

Being the largest provider of infant formula in the Third World, Nestlé became a target for all the accusations levelled against that industry by the activists. It became a symbol of 'exploitation for profit'.

Those socially concerned people in the boycott wanted Nestlé to acknowledge broad accountability for what they saw as the consequences, both direct and indirect, of its practices. They wanted Nestlé's attitude to change from what they saw as 'cool competence' to one of 'active caring'. As dialogue got under way, these perceptions did indeed change, and the way in which mutual understanding was ultimately achieved carries implications for every multinational enterprise.

As with the most modern-day social and political movements, the boycott against Nestlé was most active in the United States. Nestlé neither produces nor markets infant formula in that country, with the result that the company's main US subsidiary, the Nestlé

Company, had to bear the brunt of the boycott, even though it was not involved with the infant formula, and knew very little about it. Moreover, the Nestlé Company was, like its parent, primarily marketing oriented rather than politically oriented.

There was no unanimity of approach in the industry's handling of this problem. Nestlé could therefore count on no assistance from the major US infant formula manufacturers, who were content to let Nestlé remain isolated and handle the boycott on its own.

When the boycott started, the Nestlé Company began by talking to its critics, but this dialogue led to justifiable mistrust of the activist leadership. Unfortunately, the company then assumed that none of the critics had a legitimate case, and concentrated on attacking the tactics and motives of the political activists. The latter were delighted to be attacked, and to respond in kind, because they had established a foundation which made the most implausible accusations against Nestlé seem credible, whereas Nestlé had never established any relationship or demonstrated concern about the issues in a way that might cause the general public to give its responses a hearing.

If Nestlé had not adopted a new strategy and outlook in dealing with this issue, it would still be exchanging charges and counter-charges with the activists. Any marketing changes would have been perceived as insufficient to persuade the religious groups to modify their stance. The boycott would now still be in full force. But Nestlé's rate of change accelerated, and the company continued to change even more as it and the socially concerned began to respond to each other, and eventually to trust each other.

By late 1980, Nestlé had decided that orthodox public relations and legal responses were not effective, and that a fresh, well-coordinated international public affairs approach was needed. It made the key decision to establish early in 1981, not a boycott office, but a company, the Nestlé Coordination Center for Nutrition, Inc, (NCCN) based in Washington DC. Its purpose was to coordinate a number of nutrition research activities in North America, and also to pull together, from around the world, for dissemination throughout the western hemisphere, all the available information on nutrition projects aimed specifically at bettering the health of Third World mothers and children being carried out under the company's direction or with its support. It was also to handle the Nestlé boycott problem.

NCCN brought together, as employees or consultants, scientists with experience in Third World nutrition problems; experts with political and international public-issue backgrounds; and people with experience in working with such socially concerned people as religious leaders, teachers, home economists and health care professionals. As part of its coordination work, NCCN saw the need for Nestlé to approach the many political and social environments around it with the same creative awareness that the company brought to its successful international activities.

NCCN's first public issue activity was to listen carefully, with new sensitivity, to all the voices shouting at the company. It began to understand that these voices represented different constituencies with different priorities. NCCN soon identified two major voices. First there were the political activists — many of whom wanted to help the world's poorer mothers and children, but primarily as part of a so-called 'new international economic order' in which existing wealth would be redistributed and new international authorities would control international commerce. Then there were the religious and persons of conscience — some of whom were against the concept of profit as a primary motivator of creative economic activity, and gave a higher priority to influencing multinational companies to work to benefit the Third World's poor.

It was after a brief period of intense, careful listening,

and delineating these two major voices, that Nestlé decided on a fundamental new strategy of cooperating with its critics of conscience. At the same time, the company refused to engage in a mud-slinging contest with the ideologues and politically motivated activists. It decided instead to defer further dialogue with them until it had first achieved mutual trust with its more moderate critics.

One important truth that Nestlé was not able effectively to convey to the public was the fact that the company had been modifying its policy with respect to infant formula marketing long before it became a political issue.

Two events occurred within a few months of each other in late 1980 and early 1981, at about the time Nestlé was reviewing its policy towards the critics and establishing NCCN, that made possible a more rapid and effective implementation of the new policy of constructive cooperation than anyone originally could have thought possible.

First, the United Methodist Church, one of the largest, most respected, socially active and morally concerned religious bodies in the United States, voted to form a task force to ascertain the facts concerning Nestlé's marketing practices, and to recommend within two years (by late 1982) whether or not the Methodists should join the boycott. Most of the members of the task force were church people and theologians who were frankly dubious about Nestlé's practices, and openly inclined to join the boycott. But they were religious people of conscience, genuinely concerned about the poor, and committed to a dialogue with Nestlé, if such a dialogue could produce positive answers to the infant formula question. The company thus had a body of concerned critics it could talk with — if it were sensitive, caring and intelligent enough to do so.

Second, the World Health Assembly in Geneva passed, in May 1981, a Recommended Code of Marketing of

Breastmilk Substitutes to be used as guidelines by member states. Nestlé immediately issued a statement in Switzerland supporting the 'aim and principle' of the Code, and reaffirmed that support a month later in testimony before a US Congressional hearing in Washington.

The Methodists and Nestlé realised simultaneously that the Recommended Code provided them with a framework they could agree on and within which they could discuss Nestlé's practices.

Eighteen months of intense negotiation began. Nestlé decided that the situation required taking risks to convince the Task Force of the company's willingness to open up its attitudes and modify its practices. It gave the Task Force a large number of sensitive internal documents, so that it could follow and ascertain the company's willingness to respond positively to constructive criticism. Although the documents gave the initially hostile critics a strong new weapon that could have been used to hurt the company, the confidences were kept, and used as a basis for sharp questioning by the Task Force.

Nestlé's response was to submit a detailed aide mémoire, which was followed by others later, spelling out the steps which already had been taken to work with sovereign nations to adopt national codes, and committing the company to finding a way to implement the Code while respecting national sovereignty.

On 12 February, 1982, the two most senior Nestlé executives, Helmut Maucher, the new managing director, and Dr Carl L Angst, executive vice president, flew to Dayton, Ohio to meet with the United Methodist Church Task Force to Infant Formula. The meeting was very successful in establishing personal relationships at the highest level and in reassuring the Methodists that Nestlé's stated commitments were supported by the management in the company. That meeting was a most important benchmark in the controversy.

Some time later, the new head of the National Council

of Churches (a former member of the UMC Task Force on Infant Formula) flew to Switzerland and met there with top Nestlé management to express very directly to the company the concerns of objective church leaders and to receive assurance of the company's commitment to the WHO Code. That visit was very successful in dispelling finally several lingering misconceptions on both sides. An important, honourable, and credible bridge was built between the antagonists.

Then, in March 1982, since few nations had taken concrete steps to implement the WHO Recommendations, Nestlé issued detailed instructions to all of its managers in Third World markets requiring unilateral compliance with the Recommended Code in all nations that had not as yet promulgated national codes of their own. At the same time, Nestlé wrote to the ministers of health in every nation in which the company marketed infant formula pledging to respect national sovereignty and to obey any national code, when adopted. The company had adopted by then the policy that it would apply in the countries of the Third World its instructions if they were more stringent than national codes. Otherwise, national codes, when in existence, would apply.

In May, Nestlé announced creation of an independent Nestlé Infant Formula Audit Commission, consisting of church leaders, scientists and educators of unquestioned independence, expertise and integrity, and chaired by former US Secretary of State and Senator, Edmund S Muskie, to monitor its implementation of the Code, and to suggest changes in its marketing practices, as needed, to ensure their compliance with the Code.

Even though Nestlé had made a public commitment to the WHO Code process and even though the company had established stringent internal audit systems regarding compliance by field managers with the company's instructions on the Code, NCCN believed that there was a need for an external, impartial, respected group of social auditors to monitor that compliance. NCCN knew that despite the truth of the company's past arguments, Nestlé had a credibility problem (as many other multinational companies do).

NCCN recommended this unprecedented concept to management realising the serious risks involved and the fact that the company would be vulnerable to public embarrassment by any disgruntled member of the Commission. This action by Nestlé has been described by many scholars and journalists as 'a truly unprecedented move in the annals of corporate history'.

As a result of the steps taken by Nestlé, the highest coordinating body of the Methodist Church (the General Council on Ministries) voted to accept the Task Force's recommendation to stay out of the boycott and, through 1983 and early 1984, other churches did the same. On advice from the Task Force and the Audit Commission, Nestlé further tightened its practices. Notice was sent to Nestlé managers worldwide that the Muskie Commission members would make unannounced visits to countries of their choice to investigate and monitor compliance with the instructions on the WHO Code. It is to Nestlé's credit that it assumed these inherent risks and adopted this revolutionary concept in social audit.

During this eighteen-month period, Nestlé avoided further non-constructive confrontations with political activists. Instead, it concentrated on establishing relations with other concerned groups in the same way that it had with the Methodists.

In January 1983, the major union supporting the boycott, the American Federation of Teachers, voted to rescind its boycott. That union, and the *Washington Post*, which had supported the boycott vigorously, both suggested that Nestlé had overcome legitimate objections to its past practices, and that it was time to move on to other issues. In view of these developments, Monsignor R G Peters, publisher of the *Catholic Post*, expressed concern that the boycotters' continued intransigence would make it easy for people to believe that perhaps the thrill of the boycott had come to mean more than its original goal.

Then, Sister Regina Murphy, head of the International Nestlé Boycott Committee (INBC) questioned whether her own organization was keeping the boycott going for its own sake, as suggested in the *Catholic Post*.

By that time, many church leaders were seriously questioning the ethical and moral base for continuing a boycott against a company which — according to Dr Philip Woaman, head of the United Methodist Infant Formula Task Force — 'may be in better compliance with the . . . code than the church's hospitals'. As more and more church groups and individual leaders came to trust Nestlé, they advised INBC that the time was right for a final effort to resolve those differences remaining on interpretation of some ambiguous provisions of the Recommended Code.

The INBC narrowed those differences to four provisions of the Code that had proved difficult for Nestlé or the Muskie Commission to define adequately. A letter was sent from INBC to Nestlé announcing that if these four points could be resolved, the boycott could end. A series of low-key meetings to lay the groundwork for formal discussions between Nestlé and INBC leaders followed, including a chance meeting in December 1983 between an NCCN executive and a boycott leader on a train. Both sides agreed that the differences had become minimal. Nestlé suggested that UNICEF and WHO should resolve these remaining differing interpretations.

WHO's advice was accordingly obtained and UNICEF agreed to host a series of meetings in January 1984, at which agreement was reached on a 'Statement of Understanding', detailing Nestlé's proposal for dealing with the four points raised by INBC. As a result, a joint statement was signed by Nestlé and INBC in New York on 24 January, 1984, effectively putting an end to the long, pervasive, and at times hostile confrontation.

Thankfully the majority of corporate crises are, in

themselves, short-lived affairs (although their impact on the organization may be longer). The mismanagement of a crisis in the early stages, however, can contribute significantly to its duration and severity — as is clearly shown by the Nestlé experience.

Again, we can add some simple, but crucially important, lessons from the Nestlé boycott when formulating an approach to crisis management.

9 *Know your audience and listen to their grievances.* Critics of business are rarely, in my view, made up from the lunatic fringes. Although sometimes motivated by selfish aims, their grievances are generally either genuine or formed as a result of poor communications by the target organization. Know who your potential critics are and maintain a dialogue with them.

10 *Get your opponents on your side by getting them involved in resolving the problem.* Particularly in a protracted crisis, the sooner you can involve your critics in helping to tackle the perceived problem (and provided you act on their sensible recommendations), the more speedily you are likely to win them over and resolve the crisis.

11 *Add credibility to your cause by inviting objective, authoritative bodies to help end the crisis.* The 'sting' has been taken out of many a crisis by open cooperation with respected bodies clearly seen to be taking an unbiased view.

12 *In communicating about a crisis, avoid the use of jargon. Use language that shows you care about what has happened and which clearly demonstrates that you are trying to put matters right.* Nestlé's cold scientific and legal responses, in the early stages of the boycott, gave the impression of intransigence

31

rather than the care and concern that was no doubt felt but which the company failed to communicate.

A good example of bringing in independent, respected experts to support an argument was demonstrated by Lever Brothers, manufacturers of Persil.

How Persil had to be washed-whiter-than-white

The middle of 1983 saw the disappearance from supermarket shelves of Persil Automatic washing powder, a victim of changing washing habits and advancing technology. In its place was the new, super, better-washing, enzyme-based New System Persil Automatic. It was a product intended to give Lever Brothers an even bigger share of the market.

For a time it did. The powder's share of the huge low suds market soared from 38 per cent to 50 per cent. Then came newspaper and television stories linking the new powder with skin problems, and the consumer exodus began. Independent tests by dermatologists confirmed that the powder was not the villain it was made out to be. But by glossing over the new enzyme ingredient, Lever had produced results which were worse than anyone could have foreseen. The combination of two factors — bringing out the new formula without explaining what it was, and the high incidence of consumers who were worried, rightly or not, about biological powders, proved to be a grave mistake.

The first intimation of problems came with a *Guardian* story reporting that the National Eczema Society was no longer recommending the powder. Then the *Sunday Mirror* splashed, 'Washday alert on powder'. The following day, the *Daily Mirror* proclaimed, 'The big itch in your soap powder'. Market share plunged.

Research showed that the majority of people did not

believe what they were reading. What they needed was reassurance. A testimonial approach was used. Doorstep leaflet drops referred to 'over five million housewives' who had discovered that New System Persil Automatic was the 'best powder for today's wash'. Advertisements in provincial newspapers extolled the product and asked for comments. Resulting endorsement letters were used in ten regionalized leaflets.

TV advertising took the same approach. The original commercial was re-edited to include housewife endorsements. Dermatologists issued a summary of their findings. They considered that 0.01 per cent of those surveyed 'possibly had symptoms which might be related to New System Persil Automatic'. They concluded that 'the situation . . . seems to be comparable to that of other consumer products where a small percentage of the population appears to be intolerant'.

However, the same day, Lever Brothers announced that the old powder — relabelled 'Original Non Biological Persil Automatic' was coming back 'in response to consumer demand'. Furthermore, New System Persil would carry a prominent declaration that it was biological. Market share was recaptured.

Arranging independent tests by dermatolgists clearly played a crucial role in supporting the Persil case; equally important, however, was the use of research. How natural it would have been for Lever Brothers to assume that people were really believing what they were reading. After all, the National Eczema Society had reportedly condemned the product. Research provided the vital clue and gave direction to the company's response tactics: the public wanted reassurance. Usually, of course, there is no time to conduct research in a crisis — except in prolonged cases. Intermittent research, however, conducted during periods of normal business activity can provide an invaluable signpost to attitudes about a company, its industry, products and services and contribute towards anticipating potential trouble spots — as well as providing much additional competitive data. This leads us to a further important rule of crisis management:

13 *Know your audiences, but ensure that you have a clear picture of their grievances against you. If possible, use research to verify your beliefs.*

Sweetmail

A relatively new form of crisis with which your organization may be faced is termed 'sweetmail'. Here are some examples.

On Friday 20 June 1986 four men were arrested — three in London and one in Norwich — after a two-month undercover operation called 'Operation Feather'. Bernard Mathews, famous for his 'bootiful' turkey television commercials, had been told that unless his company handed over £50,000, deadly thallous acetate would be injected into his turkeys. There is no known antidote to the poison which would certainly have killed anyone eating a contaminated bird. The extortionists made their demands in messages sent to Mr Mathews' home in Norfolk. Operation Feather was launched after the first threat was made in a letter to Mr Mathews in April that year. According to reports, this first threat was followed by two phone calls and another letter, containing a specimen of the poison. An initial payment of £2,500 was made to the gang to lure them into an elaborate police trap. A watch was kept on banks and building society offices throughout the country. A round-the-clock check was maintained on cash machines in some areas after the gang demanded £25,000. Eventually the four men were arrested after an attempt to grab some of the ransom cash.

The police said: 'The gang tried to devise a simple but fairly new method of obtaining money.' In fact, 'sweetmailers' have been operating for some years, attempting to squeeze millions out of manufacturers and store chains by poisoning food and drink.

The problem is greatest in Japan where one sweet-mailer, dubbed 'the man with 21 faces', has extracted a fortune from firms by adding poison to sweets. In the UK, fanatics have injected chickens and turkeys with mercury and contaminated Mars bars with rat poison. They have spiked soft drinks and mouth wash — and threatened to poison oranges and put bleach into baby oil. Bleach, added to Cinzano served at a Cambridgeshire pub, caused the painful, lingering death of a woman early in March 1986.

Although British industry is reluctant to admit how successful sweetmailers have been, it is believed they have extorted substantial sums from a number of companies. Just before Christmas in 1984, fifty turkeys were removed from a Grimsby butcher after mercury was discovered in one bird. Animal liberationists claimed responsibility. The same group admitted lacing Mars bars with rat poison. Hundreds of baby oil bottles were recalled after police warned they might have been spiked with bleach in chemist shops in Hampshire; in Ulster, Loyalists were accused of planting poison in food store products to ensure 'donations' to their cause; South African oranges were claimed to have been poisoned in Birmingham as an anti-apartheid protest in 1985. Sweet-mail is on the increase.

Any form of physical crisis faced by an organization is likely to involve the police — but never more so than when threats or extortion demands are made against it. Again, the key here is to be prepared — think through the areas of your business most vulnerable to attack from outside groups and plan your response. In drawing up your contingency plans talk to the relevant officers at Scotland Yard, and other experts external to your organization, who have experience in dealing with such situations. Seek their advice and input to your own planning process.

14 *Whenever possible, seek outside expert advice when drawing up crisis contingency plans. Don't reinvent the wheel.*

How 'no comment' leads to plenty

The leak of radioactive vapour from the nuclear waste reprocessing plant in Sellafield, Cumbria, prompted one official to remark casually: 'This sort of thing happens every day in industry.' He was referring mainly to the chemical industry, where tragedies like Bhopal and, here in the UK, Flixborough, have overshadowed minor leaks which, while sometimes causing a local storm, often go unnoticed at national level. Public awareness of the dangers associated with all forms of pollution, brought sharply into focus by both Chernobyl and Bhopal, is set to change that.

Problems associated with pollution are often among the most difficult to deal with because they tend to be prolonged. An airline crash which kills all three hundred people on board is headline news for a couple of days, but is then relegated to the inside pages. Pollution, or any form of prolonged danger, can remain in the headlines for weeks, putting companies at the centre of such a crisis under almost intolerable pressure. The longer a crisis continues, the more room there is for error.

Following the explosion and fire at the Russian nuclear reactor at Chernobyl, many of the long-term implications will take months, if not years to sort out. In some countries, for example Sweden and West Germany, the full effects of the disaster may not be known until the next century. Opinion polls throughout Europe, taken a few weeks after Chernobyl, showed sharp swings against nuclear power, with some 60 to 70 per cent of voters opposing it in many countries.

Public opinion may swing back to the centre, but in most countries of Europe and in the US, the nuclear industry has much more than a propoganda job to do. The public has fastened on to the fact that, however superior Western safety systems may be, the vast concrete domes round modern reactors would not be certain to contain a Chernobyl-type explosion. The question, 'How safe is safe?' is firmly back on the agenda and is provoking wide-ranging arguments as to whether current technologies are really appropriate. In the post-Chernobyl world, future expansion by the nuclear industry will be difficult. Companies who pollute will no longer be tolerated.

A pollution problem, or any form of prolonged crisis which keeps a company unfavourably in the public eye for extended periods, places a heavy requirement on management time not only in dealing with the problem, but in responding to the hundreds of requests for information that will be received about what has gone wrong. Failure to respond adequately will make the company appear secretive, and guilty by implication. Teams of specially trained staff may be needed to man telephone lines to respond to calls from the media, environmental pressure groups, employees, local community groups and others. Senior management will need to be trained in techniques for appearing on television, being interviewed on radio and holding press conferences. This introduces another important rule:

15 *Training: As an integral part of planning to deal with a crisis, investigate what specialized training programmes may be necessary to ensure you have a professional group of people around you handling the company's external communications.* Remember also that if you operate in an industry more likely to be subject to a crisis of a prolonged nature, you may

need alternate teams which can relieve one another. More than one team may need to be trained.

Facing up to a crisis

Crises often represent turning points in organizational life. They present opportunities to establish a reputation for competence, to shape the organization and to tackle important issues. In most crises, because time is at a premium and resource allocation is critical, company executives need strategic guidelines for deciding what kinds of action are needed.

Taking action in a crisis can be fraught with risk. A strategy is needed for deciding when to define a situation as a crisis, when to take action and how to work with others in solving the crisis. Such a strategic sense is in itself a great advantage when tension develops. The ability to keep cool when everything is collapsing is a quality valued in leaders, especially since apparent confidence by the leader is so reassuring to subordinates. Such confidence, however, can only develop from adequate planning. Advance planning makes it more possible to concentrate on the actual problem when it peaks, and provides a framework for action.

Crisis management is about seizing the initiative — taking control of what has happened before it engulfs the company. Planning for a crisis is the key to corporate survival.

Initial points to consider when planning for a crisis

1   *Faced with disaster, consider the worst possible scenario — and act accordingly.*

2 *When the dust has settled, look to see what lessons you might be able to teach the rest of industry from your experience — and act accordingly.*

3 *Have a crisis management plan.*

4 *Be prepared to demonstrate human concern for what has happened.*

5 *In communications terms, be prepared to seize early initiatives by rapidly establishing the company as the single authoritative source of information about what has gone wrong and what steps the organization is taking to remedy the situation.*

6 *Whenever possible, look for ways of using the media as part of your armoury for containing the effects of the crisis.*

7 *At the outset of a crisis, quickly establish a 'war room', or Emergency Control Centre and staff it with senior personnel trained to fulfill specific roles designed to contain and manage the crisis.*

8 *Set up telephone hotlines to cope with the flood of additional incoming calls that will be received during a crisis. Have personnel trained to man the hotlines.*

9 *Know your audience and listen to their grievances.*

10 *Get your opponents on your side by getting them involved in resolving the problem.*

11 *Add credibility to your cause by inviting objective, authoritative bodies to help end the crisis.*

12 *In communicating about crisis, avoid the use of jargon. Use language that shows you care about what has happened and which clearly demonstrates that you are trying to put matters right.*

13 *Know your audiences, but ensure that you have a clear picture of their grievances against you. If possible, use research to verify your beliefs.*

14 *Whenever possible, seek outside expert advice when drawing up crisis contingency plans. Don't reinvent the wheel.*

15 *Training: As an integral part of planning to deal with crisis, look at what specialized training programmes may be required to ensure you have a professional group of people around you handling the company's external communications.*

Bibliography and references

Robert Levy, 'Crisis Public Relations', *Dun's Business Month*, August 1983.

Leonard J Snyder, 'After Tylenol: A Critique and Second Opinion', *International Public Relations Review*, August 1983.

Eric Clark, 'Persil Comes Out of the Spin', *Marketing*, July 26, 1984.

Simon Jones, 'Why all executives should learn crisis management', *Marketing Week*, November 5, 1982.

Professor David Kuechle, 'Crisis management: an executive quagmire', *Business Quarterly*, Spring 1985.

Rafael D Pagan Jr, 'Resolving the Nestlé boycott', *International Public Relations Review*, August 1984.

CHAPTER 2

The Anatomy of a Crisis

Regrettably, there are further types of crisis which can arise, rapidly and without warning, to disrupt the smooth running of our day-to-day business lives.

A crisis, it seems, is always caused either by people or machines. This chapter looks at examples from both groups and suggests some preventative measures which can be put in place.

The chance of becoming a terrorist target except in certain countries like Northern Ireland, is related to the size and nature of the organization for which you work. But the possibility that a breakdown of the new technology you have recently installed will cause sufficient disorder to kill your company, whatever its size, poses a threat which only the foolhardy would ignore.

The terrorist threat

It was a balmy day in Buenos Aires on 6 December 1973, when Victor Samuelson, the 36-year-old manager of Exxon Corporation's Campana refinery outside the city, was entertaining business guests. After lunch at the Esso Club, adjacent to the refinery, Mr Samuelson took one guest, an Exxon official from the US, outside to see the club's grounds.

As the two men strolled toward the swimming pool, someone shouted at them in Spanish: 'Don't go any further; the place is surrounded. Go back inside.' The two re-entered the club building to find a dozen armed men, some of them wearing stocking masks. Two grabbed

Mr Samuelson, kicked him in the side, pushed him outside and forced him on to the floor of a waiting car, which then sped off.

The kidnapping was the beginning of nearly five months of terror for Mr Samuelson, and anguish for his family and numerous Exxon officials ranging from a company public relations man in Buenos Aires to the chairman of the board in New York. Mr Samuelson's life was threatened; Exxon was told bombs might be planted at its service stations throughout Argentina; and one Exxon official was told he himself might be machine-gunned. In the end, after hair-raising negotiations for Mr Samuelson's release, he was ransomed. Exxon paid the abductors $14.2 million.

The story of Mr Samuelson's kidnapping raises the spectre of one of the most difficult kinds of corporate crises — involving threats to the lives of corporate officers, employees, representatives and their families. In the last decade, multinational corporations have become the principal target of terrorist organizations. While the number of worldwide terrorist incidents fluctuates from year to year, in 75 per cent of all terrorist incidents US and West European nationals have been the targets. According to US Department of State figures, 40 per cent of all attacks are directed at business executives and private individuals.

Although considered less newsworthy these days, terrorist attacks have increased steadily since 1968 — and nowhere more so than in Western Europe, with over 1,200 between 1968 and 1979. They have also become more lethal. As target organizations increase their defences, terrorists resort to tactics such as car bombings which are harder to defend against and inflict more casualties. At the same time, terrorists must use greater force to overwhelm the defence. This point was demonstrated when Columbian guerillas killed both the bodyguards of Texaco executive Kenneth Bishop before kidnapping him.

Once, when I worked for Gulf Oil, the phone rang and the voice of a senior officer from the Corporation, based in Houston, said: 'Mike, we're activating the Crisis Management Team, (of which I was a member). Some of our people have been kidnapped. Get over to Switzerland and meet us at the Montreux Palace Hotel tomorrow.' The next day the rest of the Crisis Management Team arrived in Montreux from the US — two corporate security officials who looked like sumo wrestlers in suits, a lawyer, an employee relations expert and a senior vice-president. We were told that some employees working in Angola had been kidnapped by one of the revolutionary groups there; they were being held for ransom and we were to wait in Montreux until a representative from the group arrived to carry out the negotiations.

As we waited, we considered every possible scenario and what actions we should take in each situation. Of paramount importance was the safety of our employees. We knew that the US government would not negotiate with terrorists on behalf of multinational corporations (on the grounds that involvement of government officials only serves to encourage terrorists to commit more crimes in their quest for recognition, publicity and money). We also knew we couldn't count on much practical support from the Angola government. We had to deal with the situation ourselves. Having thought through our responses to every conceivable demand they might make, we waited — and waited.

The sumo wrestlers told us we couldn't leave the hotel, in case a kidnap attempt was made on one of us; and we had to stick in pairs when moving around the hotel.

Eight days later we received a telephone call from the corporation's senior representative in Angola saying the terrorists' representatives had been unable to obtain exit visas and had therefore released the employees that morning! They were picked up wandering around the jungle. Fortunately, a happy ending.

That Gulf Oil, Exxon and Texaco should have been

picked as terrorist targets is supported by statistics which show that targets tend to be oil companies, banks, overseas construction firms and multinational corporations that represent the 'western' (especially American) way of life, like credit card companies, Coca-Cola, MacDonalds and others. The heart of the problem is that the international business community has nowhere to look but to itself for protection. Governments have not provided effective protection against the terrorist threat for business. Quite apart from the operational and emotional difficulties posed, terrorism also makes a considerable impact on a corporation's bottom line. According to one US research firm, private spending on security equipment and services in the US alone will reach $50 billion by 1990.

A joint study by Harvard and Yale universities showed that multinationals spend over $2 billion internationally to protect their assets from threats of political violence. Protective measures are generally reactive. After the Ponto and Schleyer killings, over $1 billion was spent to enhance the security of other West German business leaders. Multinational corporations are estimated to spend over $80 million annually in kidnap and ransom insurance premiums.

It has been calculated that at least $350 million has been paid in ransom to terrorists between 1973 and 1983. Examples include $3 million paid by Firestone in Argentina, $14.2 million paid by Exxon's Esso subsidiary in Argentina, and $10 million paid by Goodyear in Guatamala. Bombings and facility attacks have caused extensive damage to corporations and are partly responsible for the skyrocketing costs of security and insurance. In 1974, in protest against ITT's role in Chile, a warehouse and an Avis office were bombed in Italy, causing over $9 million in damages. In 1975, the offices of TWA, 3M and Coca-Cola were bombed in Paris in protest against a meeting between Presidents Gerald Ford and Valery Giscard D'Estaing. In 1978, damage estimated at $1 million was caused in one day by attacks on American companies in Nicaragua.

There are other costs too. Many corporations pay executives supplementary compensation if they are assigned to unstable locations. Coca-Cola reportedly paid its expatriate managers in Argentina a 10 per cent bonus during the most serious period of violence. In addition to these direct cost implications, doing business in a terrorist environment can have a detrimental effect on quality and productivity. Companies, particularly in high technology fields, are reluctant to put advanced equipment or key employees in hazardous places.

Restrictions on travel to turbulent countries means critical equipment often has to be shipped out for repairs, increasing downtime and costs. The relationship between multinationals and host governments can also present problems. Several corporations have encountered difficulties balancing their obligations to employees with the requirments of the host country. In Columbia, for instance, several employees of a US firm were jailed for negotiating a ransom payment. In Venezuela, the government threatened to expropriate the property of a company that had cooperated with terrorist demands. Some foreign governments now make it a crime for a company or its representative to negotiate or to pay ransom to terrorists.

Given the growing number and complexity of terrorist-induced crises — multiple demands delivered in the public spotlight, heightened emotions, threats against a variety of corporate assets, the virtual assurance of a 'no-win' situation — it is imperative that organizations are prepared. If they are not, the probability of a successful resolution is minimized. Consider also the longer term implications of being perceived to mishandle such a situation.

Any company has a variety of audiences who could be negatively influenced by an inappropriate response to terrorist demands. These audiences — shareholders, the host government, parent government, and employees, to name a few — will see the outcome of the corporate negotiations and judge the skill with which the company resolved the conflict. If the response is not decisive and does not have a positive outcome, the lack of confidence created among these critical audiences could be disastrous to the company. It may become less attractive to investors, and employees may request transfers back to the company's country of origin. Managers at home may refuse international assignments.

The business community as a whole is aware of the terrorist threat and is devoting increasing resources, often in a reactive fashion, to minimize corporate risk. Intelligence about how actual threats have been dealt with by individual companies is, however, hard to come by. Companies are wary of sharing information that might inadvertently reveal facts useful to competitors, or they may fear that disclosing threats will alarm employees and shareholders. It is always possible that one company might inadvertently reveal the extent of another's security precautions.

Small, informed groups of security professionals can and do meet regularly to exchange information. These groups usually form because of their interest in a particular geographic location or because of similar business activities and common problems.

Although it is one of the most difficult crisis areas to plan for, actions which can be taken by a company potentially faced by a terrorist threat include:

1 *Intelligence swapping:* for example, information on which banks can accommodate ransom demands, which airlines will help a released hostage leave the country quickly, which guard force will be the most reliable, or even which local security force will respond favourably to calls for assistance. All this information can prove invaluable.

Table 2.1 International terrorism incidents 1968–1979

Type	Number	%
Explosive bombings	1,588	48
Incendiary bombings	456	14
Kidnappings	263	8
Assassinations	246	7
Armed attacks	188	6
Letter bombings	186	6
Hijackings	100	3
Theft/break-ins	78	2
Barricade and hostage	73	2
Snipings	71	2
Other	87	3

Target	Number	%
Business executives/facilities	487	36
Diplomatic officials/property	273	20
Other government officials	217	16
Military officials/property	204	15
Private citizens	166	12

Source: US Department of Defense and Central Intelligence Agency

2 *Identify the targets most at risk:* it may be the home, the office, the car, it might happen while travelling, or attending public functions. It may involve family members.

3 *Maintain executive protection programmes:* these can include armoured cars, protective clothing, electronic security counter measures, residential security systems/alarms, executive and family training, bodyguards and small arms training.

4 *Have a crisis management team:* ready to be activated at a moment's notice to deal with the situation.

5   *Evaluate 'what-if' scenarios:* again think through possible scenarios with which your organization may be faced and plan your responses to each.

American consultants Frederick Newman and Lloyd Singer developed the following terrorist scenario for ten multinational clients who had either been victims of terrorist threats or who had perceived the need for an organized response to such threats.

The simulation involved a one-day exercise to test the crisis management team's competence in handling the extortion kidnapping of a major executive of the fictitious American foods corporation, Amfocor. First news of the kidnapping is received via a five-minute tape delivered to the switchboard of Amfocor. Part of it runs as follows:

'This is communique 1 of the Peoples Armed Liberation Movement's action against corporate injustice. Today, one of our intelligence detachments has arrested a prime suspect of super crimes against the just struggles of the world's exploited masses to achieve genuine political, economic and social independence from imperialism.

'The prisoner identifies himself as Lawrence McKay with the pompous title of vice-president, one of the international capitalist conspiracy. He is under investigation by the chief judge of the people's court and a warrant specifying charges against him will be delivered in due time.

'With this act, we hereby declare open warfare on the real mafia in this imperialistic country, bloodsucking corporations and their gangster chieftains. McKay is only the first of these thugs who will know the power of the people . . .'

The luckless Lawrence McKay is the 50-year old general manager of Amfocor's chemical division. The simulation then opens with a film which shows the events leading up to the Lawrence McKay kidnap, and the first two meetings of the Amfocor crisis management team. Designed to provide concentrated background information on the incident and build the sense of emotional intensity and urgency needed for realism, the film also reduces the amount of time necessary to set the stage and get the exercise rolling.

At a dramatic point in the film, the screen goes black and the 'real' crisis management team goes into action. The group tackles a problem that involves a set of complex ransom demands; a distressed Mrs McKay who wants to appear on television; and Amfocor's Chairman, who insists on inserting his limited expertise at crucial points in team deliberations. The simulation includes the press conferences, newspaper advertisements, cash and non-cash ransom demands, radio broadcasts, additional messages from the terrorists through an intermediary, medical problems with the victim and liaison with various authorities. To increase the pressure, the simulation is run against clocks that shrink time by a 3:1 ratio, giving 20 minutes to one hour (a powerful stress generator).

Four types of material are used in the simulation:

1 The basic background kit, which provides corporate, victim and terrorist information necessary to start the simulation.

2 On-request background material, giving information available only when requested by the crisis management team, a challenge to the information-gathering and analytical ability of the team.

3 Pre-programmed materials: formal, timed memos, telephone calls, tapes etc, which form the backbone of the exercise.

4 Stimulators: ad hoc materials, which are generally tailor-made and designed to stimulate and challenge the crisis management team.

Changes in team membership frequently happen as a result of running a simulation. Additions and deletions of certain functions for handling terrorist incidents are common. Outside experts in psychiatry, terrorist nego-tiation, threat analysis, and political analysis are common additions. Later, we shall look in more detail at how to plan against a crisis ever taking place. Prevention is always better than cure. But first, it's worth considering the implications of two other forms of corporate crisis: computer breakdown and the threat of being taken over by an unwanted company. Handling unwanted takeover bids is dealt with separately in Chapter 4.

Computer catastrophe

The dependence which people in business place on computer technology is already awesome — and, for many of us, the working of that technology remains a great mystery. But the implications to business of a prolonged computer system breakdown, denying oper-ational management vital information, is equally awesome. Such a breakdown puts into question the survival of the entire organization, exposing it to an unacceptable business risk.

Many of us followed the halting start with which the London Stock Exchange introduced new technology to facilitate the 'Big Bang' in October 1986. More than once, the ability of the Stock Exchange to continue to provide the service for which it is designed was called into ques-tion because of the problems it encountered in harnessing the new technology. For example, on 14 March 1986, it issued the following news release:

'Contract volume in the Traded Options Market has trebled since last September. To accommodate this sharp increase the Stock Exchange yesterday introduced a new computerized matching system. Despite previous trials, the new system developed hardware faults when put into operation, seriously delaying the processing of yesterday's bargains.

'Although the faults have now been identified, the Stock Exchange decided that the outstanding bargains should be cleared before normal trading resumes. To allow time for this to take place it was decided with regret not to open the Traded Options Market today except for Currency Options which are cleared on a different basis.

'It is anticipated that the Market will re-open on Monday, 17 March.'

'Anger as Traded Options Market Fails to Open' said the headline in *The Times* the following day. Describing the Stock Exchange statement as 'terse', the newspaper's report said that the credibility of the London Traded Options Market suffered a serious setback when it remained closed all day, making it the third time dealings had been disrupted in that month.

After the computer system failed the Stock Exchange Options Committee immediately went into emergency session to discuss the Exchange's legal position in the face of possible claims for compensation. In the end, members of the Options Committee took the view that the Exchange could not be sued for losses sustained by investors. They also felt that it would be difficult for investors to establish that they had lost money because of the closure. However, the breakdown of the computerized system led investors to doubt the ability of the clearing system to cope with record levels of bargains struck in the market. Brokers and fund managers wanted a full explanation from the Stock Exchange which would reassure investors that the situation would not happen again.

The *Sunday Times* really hit the nail on the head when it said: 'Friday's closure of the Traded Options Market for the second time in a month undermines the credibility of the Stock Exchange. This sort of collapse is dangerous in a purely electronic market. The Traded Options Market could go anywhere. If systems are better overseas, then that is where it will end up.'

And that, ultimately, is the likely consequence of prolonged or regular computer failure. Customers will go elsewhere where the service is more efficient. Most companies maintain their most important records on a computer. The prevailing trend is for even greater dependence on electronic data processing in both the commercial and industrial fields as managements strive for the competitive edge. The day-to-day operations of companies depend on electronic processing of transactions, financial and regulatory reports, customer service support, telecommunications and payroll preparation. Even the complex decisions associated with the managing of an organization — planning, scheduling, budgeting, production and distribution — rely on electronic data processing.

While no chief executive could accept prolonged cessation of data processing, nagging questions of vulnerability to unlikely disruptive events, the level of exposure, and the ability of the system to recover are often left unanswered. Questions to be asked of the consequences of computer failure include:

1   How would essential operations be sustained?

2   Which business functions would suffer most?

3   During what period would recovery be effected?

4   What is the potential cost of recovery and reconstruction?

As always, contingency planning can help an executive answer these questions. Every computer facility needs to be prepared for such events as a ten-minute power failure, which is possible and probable, and could not be considered an unlikely event. Short-term security and back-up recovery plans should be enforced during such failures. Back-up plans are not, however, contingency plans. They assume that normal operations will resume after the event within a relatively short period. Contingency plans need to focus on events that halt normal operations for a longer time. Such plans must provide for:

1 Resumption of processing critical applications within a defined, short-term interval.

2 Restoration of total processing and return to standard operating procedures.

The requirements of the plan should be defined by determining both the organization's needs and the time required to restart processing after a disaster. The organization needs to understand, for each application, the loss it would sustain from operating without a particular system over a given period of time.

Plans should describe the critical resources needed to recover lost data and specify time frames for the availability of those resources. Certainly, the more time available to produce critical resources after a disaster, the easier and less expensive for an organization to recover. The time element, therefore, must be realistically assessed and specific plans for obtaining each resource must be documented. The plan must define assigned responsibility for:

1 Identifying and monitoring critical operations.

2 Providing specific resources.

3 Monitoring and testing readiness.

4 Executing the plan.

5 Updating and maintaining the plan.

Monitoring and testing are probably the most critical elements of preparation, because there is no feedback on plan effectiveness until the unlikely event occurs. To summarize, contingency planning for dealing with computer breakdown should take into account:

1 *How would essential operations be sustained?*

2 *Which business functions would suffer most?*

3 *During what period would recovery be effected?*

4 *What is the potential cost of recovery and reconstruction?*

5 *What loss would be incurred from operating without a particular system over a given period of time?*

6 *What critical resources would be needed to recover lost data?*

7 *How quickly could such resources be assembled?*

8 *From where would they be obtained?*

Bibliography and references

'*Patterns of International Terrorism: 1981*', Office for Combatting Terrorism, US Department of State, July 1982.

Joseph S Schneider, 'Business as a Terrorist Target', *Security Management*, May 1984.

Frederick H Newman and Lloyd W Singer, 'Simulation—A Key to Crisis Management Training', *Security Management*, September 1982.

William M Cauley, 'A Secret Exxon Report Shows how a Company Handled a Kidnapping', *The Wall Street Journal*, December 1983.

Paul Okkerse, 'A Total Computer Disaster', *Rydge's*, December 1982.

CHAPTER 3

Planning for the Unexpected

So, what constitutes a corporate crisis, potentially threatening the lifeblood of an organization, can take many forms. Yet the rules for surviving the unexpected, whether physical, financial, idealogical or political in origin, are broadly the same. They have been proven time and again.

If planning for crisis is the key to corporate survival, you need to know how to plan and how to test your plans to ensure they would really work in a crisis situation. But first, you need to develop a positive attitude to crisis planning. Why?

Those who are alert to the possibility that any event, even a crisis, is an opportunity to gain friends, to enlist support and, possibly, to attract new customers or shareholders, are well prepared to seize the initiative. Failure to have in place well-tried and tested contingency plans for every kind of emergency means that, when the unexpected does occur, the company can only assume a combative posture; it is, of necessity, put into a defensive frame of mind. Assuming a primarily defensive position establishes a negative attitude. It focusses thinking on reacting to conditions instead of the company acting on its own initiative. When a whole company is put into a negative frame of mind it is virtually certain to be seen as arrogant and unsympathetic to others, as witness the Nestlé boycott. Instead, when positioned to deal not only with the crisis but also the inherent opportunities, a proactive posture can be established which leads to a positive attitude rather than a seige mentality.

Actions speak louder than words

A second principle, perhaps of even greater importance, is that deeds build a reputation far more effectively than words in advertisements or glossy brochures. In today's climate of corporate accountability, promises — words alone — are greeted with cynicism or disbelief. Such an approach actually creates a target for attack should the slightest lapse in performance occur. Nothing gladdens the public heart so much as a fall from grace by the excessively righteous. Self-aggrandisement campaigns lack credibility because everyone knows the sponsor accentuates the beauty spots and hides the warts.

A record of responsible deeds is a vital ingredient for a positive image. The essence of a good reputation rests not in trying to conjure up a good story to cover up substandard performance, but in sensitising management to the need to adjust performance so that the deeds speak for themselves. The guiding principles of crisis planning are to:

1 Develop a positive attitude towards crisis management.

2 Bring performance throughout the organization into line with public expectation. Build credibility through a succession of responsible deeds.

3 Seek and act on the opportunities during a crisis.

It boils down to deeds versus declarations. A record of responsible deeds is the organization's insurance policy when, and if, something does go wrong. All this depends, of course, on top management commitment. Without it, all the best intentions of individuals like the public relations manager, the safety manager, the employee relations manager or the financial manager will be fruitless.

Regrettably, it often takes a major corporate disaster, or simply a series of mistakes — both of which can leave a legacy of far-reaching damage to the organization — before the corporate culture is adjusted from responsive to proactive. Although in an increasing number of organizations, executives no longer view a crisis as something beyond their control — they have devised new crisis management plans and set up specially-trained teams that can swing into action when disaster strikes — most companies remain very poorly prepared for crisis, as Stephen Fink's survey among chief executives in the United States has shown. (Figures for the United Kingdom are not available but are likely to be even worse.)

A coherent approach to planning

The principles applying to crisis management planning are broadly the same for virtually all types of corporate crisis, and the methods for implementing the plan will not vary greatly for different types of crisis. No one can anticipate every crisis that might conceivably arise, but there are a number of steps every company can take to prepare for one.

A coherent approach begins with the identification of potential crises. These include existing situations that have the potential to become crises; crises that have beset the company in the past and that might recur; and crises that are known to have beset comparable companies. For example:

- A company with wage negotiations looming ahead can anticipate the possibility of a work stoppage, and consider the potential effects of picketing and even violence.

- Companies that have continuing pollution control

problems can anticipate the possibility of incidents — for example, smoke pouring from a stack when control fails, or a breakdown in the wastewater treatment plant.

- Plant accidents involving injuries and loss of life or mine collapses are facts of industrial life.

- Product-related problems (such as revelations of poor quality or allegations of harm to consumers) are always possible and should be planned for.

The need here is to catalogue the areas of risk; to assess the risk parameters. From this starting point it becomes easier to think through the logical series of steps which need to be taken into account in the crisis planning process. Having identified the areas of risk, the next questions to ask are:

1 Does the company have policies and procedures designed to prevent a risk from turning into a crisis?

2 Do plans exist for dealing with every aspect of the crisis should it occur?

3 Have the plans been tested to ensure that they work satisfactorily?

Various supplementary, but equally important, questions may be added. For example:

4 Has the company worked out who (both inside and outside the organization) would be affected by any given crisis, and how?

5 Do plans include procedures for communicating effectively to affected groups about what has happened and what is being done about it?

6 Have the communications aspects of the plan been tested as well as the company's operational response?

In short, planning for crisis management may be summarized as:

1 *Cataloguing potential crisis situations.*

2 *Devising policies for their prevention.*

3 *Formulating strategies and tactics for dealing with each potential crisis.*

4 *Identifying who will be affected by them.*

5 *Devising effective communications channels to those affected so as to minimize damage to the organization's reputation.*

6 *Testing everything.*

Appoint a crisis management team

If you belong to that majority of the business community who believe that crisis is 'as inevitable as death or paying taxes' (why else would you be thumbing through this book?) it is fair to assume that you are planning to do something positive about the management of potential crisis within your own organization. There are really no half measures, only differences in scale according to the size and nature of the business you work in. Either way, take the bull by the horns and appoint a *crisis management team* to review, or create, the plans, policies and procedures for dealing with a crisis. These will be dictated by the business environment in which you operate. Appointment of the team will demonstrate the organization's commitment to responsible management of its business. If it does its job effectively, the team will minimize the risk of a crisis occurring in the first place, will help contain the crisis should it occur, will reduce the damage to the organization's reputation, and will change the organization's culture from responsive to positive.

Selection of the crisis management team

Various leadership styles emerge during either a crisis or crisis simulations. While the 'human', participative manager is generally the most effective crisis management team leader, he can sometimes inhibit the rapid decision-making required in an emergency. The team should be made up of relatively high-level managers or other responsible professionals carefully chosen for their personal qualities and talents (breadth of vision, the ability to stay cool, and to make swift, clearly-expressed decisions) as well as their rank, status within, and knowledge of, the organization, and the business and political environment in which it operates. On the other hand, the authoritarian leader may act decisively at the expense of the team's creative process, demotivating its members and inhibiting their creativity. It is vital for the team leader to recognize team members' different styles and values and to integrate them to maximum advantage during the crisis.

Some of the styles which may emerge include:

The 'ideas' person
A creative member who is constantly injecting new ideas and suggestions. Some of these may be far-fetched, but some may have real merit. It is vital for the leader to filter out the viable ideas and discard the 'rest' without discouraging the flow.

The communicator
The individual who helps the flow of communications both within and outside the team (not necessarily the team leader).

The doom merchant
The devil's advocate who brings out the negative aspects of each proposed idea or solution.

The bookkeeper
The neat and orderly member who wants the records and logs maintained to perfection. This individual is more comfortable in this role than as a decision-maker. Nonetheless, it is a vital role.

The humanist
The people-oriented member whose solutions always lean toward the human aspects of the problem. An important visionary in the heat of the moment.

The team should form a standing committee trained to anticipate clearly and comprehensively any type of crisis situation; to develop strategies and procedures for dealing with crisis; to check that those policies and procedures are being implemented; and to provide overall direction and counsel in the event of an actual crisis occurring.

Role of the crisis management team

1 Anticipate, clearly and comprehensively, all forms of crisis situation.

2 Develop strategies and procedures for dealing with them.

3 Check that policies and procedures are being implemented.

4   Provide overall direction and counsel during a crisis.

Cataloguing, or anticipating, crises of a physical or financial nature is often easier than addressing those of an ideological or political nature; an ideological crisis, (as in the Nestlé boycott which eventually led to widespread questioning of the validity of multinational business as a legitimate and useful force in the world), or a politically-orientated crisis (for example, the introduction of the 'windfall profit tax' on the UK banking industry), although usually slower to arise, may be equally catastrophic.

The secret lies in recognizing the nature of the external decision-making process, in knowing who are your friends and who are your foes, and in considering the possible impact of their views and decisions on the commercial viability of your organization. The views of such groups — be they the EEC, national government, political activists, civil servants, local authorities, environmentalists or others — need to be tracked, prioritized in terms of immediacy and likely damage to the organization, and plans should be laid for dealing with them.

If corporate objectives are to be met, then the company is likely to need varying degrees of support at various times from these external groups because they have either the power or the influence, or both, to affect attainment of those objectives.

Included in such a catalogue of crisis issues might be: consumer protection, technology transfer, profits repatriation, trade with South Africa, disclosure of information, worker participation, environmental protection, a change in government, or increase in terrorist attacks. The tracking process is often carried out by the association or body representing an industry sector who will then advise individual companies within that sector. Nonetheless, individual organizations need to check that their best interests are being represented by the industry body and that they are, indeed, giving consideration to or implementing the advice being given. Many organizations maintain their own issue tracking systems, either via their public relations or government relations departments or by employing specialist external consultancies. The role of these groups is not only to monitor social, economic and political thinking but to recommend strategic action to the board of directors designed to maximize opportunities, or minimize negative impact, from the likely outcome of prevailing external attitudes.

Crisis prevention

The key role of the crisis management team must be to ensure that as far as possible, a crisis does not occur. It needs to set company-wide policies appropriate to the hazards or risks of its business and to ensure that the management of each part of the business is not only given the funds or other resources required to enable it to comply with the policies, *but is also responsible for implementing them*. Such policies should go beyond ensuring that the organization complies merely with existing regulations. They should endeavour to anticipate 'worst case' scenarios. Although this approach may well prove more costly, the costs of not setting such far-reaching policies can prove catastrophic in terms of human lives and the company's entire future. Developing these policies against agreed company criteria will help to give them shape and depth. Such criteria might be developed by answering the following questions:

- Would this situation really affect our bottom line?

- How realistic is the identified potential crisis situation?

- Could corporate action halt or moderate the crisis?

- Does the policy stand up to public examination?

- Are the resources to act available?

- Is the cost to the company acceptable?

- Is the will to act present?

- What would be the effect of inaction?

A positive approach to crisis management demands that the implementation of preventative policies which have been developed is checked on a regular basis. Part of the crisis management team's remit should be to conduct audits to check policy implementation. This can be done by either undertaking such audits itself or by appointing a risk audit group, comprising at least one member of the crisis management team, a specialist in the area being studied and a suitably qualified outside consultant (to provide an objective view).

Take, for example, a manufacturing company being audited for implementation of policies to prevent a physical crisis. Each year, the audit group might select an audit programme which covers different topics — safety and loss prevention, air and water quality, solid waste disposal, occupational health and product quality. The particular sites chosen for audit could be based on their risk potential, their recent performance, and the time since they were last audited, to ensure that a good cross-section of the company is included. Each audit might last three days and concentrate on one topic to ensure that a study of the appropriate depth is conducted. To give the audit process weight, the audit teams need to meet the main board at least twice yearly and report on the status of the risk audit programme and the measures required to minimize new areas of risk which may have been identified.

Such a system, employed by numerous, more enlightened, companies in different industries, works well. It is sufficiently detached to take an objective view of each situation and ensure that appropriate, but not necessarily identical, standards can be applied across all divisions. The continuing interest displayed by the board gives authority to the crisis management team and ensures that the divisional and local management corrects the deficiencies which are identified. Above all, it can prevent a crisis situation from developing.

Auditing the implementation of policies to prevent a financial crisis involves a similar format. The risk audit group adopts the protagonist role of, for example, an unwanted bidder for the company and looks for the tell-tale signs of weakness in the company's performance which could make it an easy prey. (Chapter 4 looks at these tell-tale signs in detail.) It then reports areas of weakness to the main board with recommendations for strengthening them.

Formulating strategies and tactics for dealing with each potential crisis

Assuming that, as Murphy's Law states, 'anything that can go wrong, will go wrong', plans need to be in place for dealing with each potential crisis should it occur. These plans will begin to suggest themselves as a result of the crisis cataloguing process. In planning the company's operational response to a crisis, it is important to keep in mind the worst-scenario approach. In the aftermath, you will rarely be criticized for considering every aspect of the situation and acting accordingly. But, obviously, balanced judgement needs to prevail. Not all crises will demand the same level of response so it is important to try to define, or categorize, responses for dealing with each potential crisis situation. This applies particularly to the external communications stance adopted by the company during a crisis. Overreacting publicly (rather than operationally) may actually aggravate the situation and create a greater crisis than the original one.

For example, a local problem may have been picked up by the local press but that doesn't mean that you have to go issuing detailed statements around the world on the international wire services. You may, however, need to have such a statement on standby in case the problem escalates and interest in the problem widens. Tactics employed will always hinge on the specifics of each particular situation — in other words, it is unlikely that, when disaster strikes, the pattern will follow the exact lines of the crisis management plan. Nonetheless, it can be enormously helpful to draw up game plans, and to make them as detailed as possible. Part of those tactics may call for the formation of crisis control teams, identified by the crisis management team, and trained to handle the tactical requirements of each given crisis. The distinction between the two teams is crucial. There should be a single crisis management team that provides high-level thinking and support in any crisis situation while the crisis control teams are responsible for handling the tactical requirements of each given situation. During the crisis, the crisis management team may need to be established in a dedicated emergency control centre, or 'war room'.

A checklist of what the emergency control centre might need to contain includes:

- *An adequate number of telephones.* At least one of these should be ex-directory or capable of use for transmitting calls only. This will avoid a situation where outgoing calls cannot be made because the main switchboard is overloaded with calls from anxious relatives, press, and other external groups.

- *Adequate internal lines.*

- *Radio equipment.*

- *Plans of each installation at risk showing:*

    Locations of hazardous material

    Sources of safety equipment

    Fire-water system and alternative sources of water

    Stocks of other types of fire extinguishers

    Plant entrances and road systems, updated to indicate any road which is impassable

    Assembly points, casualty treatment centres

    Location of the plant in relation to surrounding community

- *Plans on which can be illustrated:*

    Areas affected or endangered

    Deployment of emergency vehicles and personnel

    Areas where particular problems arise, eg fractured pipe-lines

    Area evacuated

    Other relevant information

    (It helps if these plans are covered with plastic or glass sheets on which chinagraph or felt-pen markings can be made and erased as required.)

- *Note pads, pens, pencils to record messages received and any instructions for delivery by runner.*

- *Nominal roll of employees.*

- *List of key personnel, addresses and telephone numbers.*

Practicable call-up procedures need to be worked out which clearly identify who does what to what and who communicates what to whom, against each potential crisis situation. These procedures must encompass those with responsibility for an operational response, such as a plant shutdown, product response (recall, or relabelling, or both), and communications response to the outside world.

Since the unexpected has a habit of occurring outside office hours, a foolproof cascade call-out procedure is required with back-up alternatives to stand in for key individuals if they are uncontactable. (The cascade principle involves each member of the emergency team having a responsibility to call at least another two members of the team once he or she has been called.)

Facilities and hardware for implementing the call-out also need to be checked. Do key individuals require mobile telephones or bleepers, for instance? How would the organization's existing communications hardware (switchboard, telex and facsimile machines) be able to cope with the flood of additional calls and messages demanded by a crisis situation? The switchboard operators need to know whom to expect calls from under emergency conditions and to whom those calls should be routed. Clearly defined procedures have to be worked out for switchboard personnel because if they have not been told where to route calls during an emergency they will second-guess, and chaos can ensue.

Attention needs to be paid to modes of physical communication, for example can head office communi-

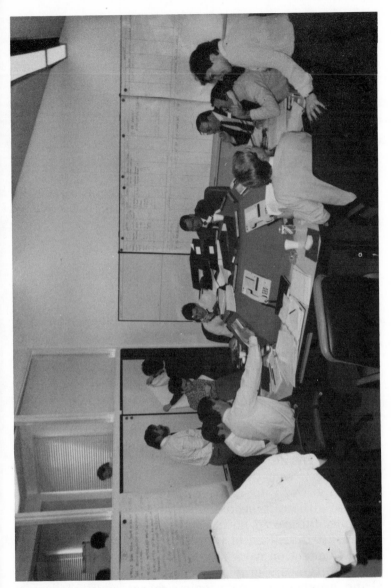

Figure 3.1: The Emergency Control Centre at Total Oil Marine's Aberdeen headquarters being tested during a simulated emergency exercise. In the top left-hand corner is the 'Quiet Room', partitioned away from the main Centre.

cate with the regional plant which has suffered an explosion if the plant's switchboard is jammed, and are there facilities for communicating in secret between one location and the other?

Does the company have emergency travel arrangements to get to the scene of the incident in the middle of the night? Where will the media be accommodated? Are photographs or film footage of the plant available?

A comprehensive checklist of all the facilities and technological hardware that would be needed to cope effectively with a crisis should be reviewed and any obvious gaps filled.

Put the plan in writing

Having carried out these checks, catalogued the risk areas, assigned responsibilities and developed the call-out procedures, everything needs to be put into writing. The importance of making written plans cannot be understated. Too often, however, plans to confront crises, if they exist at all, exist only in the minds of a few key individuals. Companies must overcome the 'don't worry about it because Bill will know what to do if it happens' syndrome. Bill may be on holiday, or dead. Even if he is available, he will be too busy to explain plans that should be readily available to all concerned.

The absence of the written plan can cause hours of additional work to an already fraught management because without it, people forget to take key actions. For example, failure to notify employees in an emergency can result in a flood of telephone calls about the effect of the incident on work schedules. Valuable time can be lost, and tempers grow short, because names and telephone numbers of key people are not available when they are needed. Checklists of things to do and people to contact are invaluable. When the situation is chaotic, it's a blessing to be able to hand to subordinates lists of

74

things to do, giving assurance that all the essential steps will be taken.

The plan should not be too rigid and specific, however, nor too long. It should provide the flexibility which acknowledges the unpredictable aspects of any crisis situation, but which gives management leeway to use common sense. It needs a structure, but a loose structure. Put the plan in writing and distribute it to key managers. Having prepared a written crisis management plan, it will need regular updating — not a problem if someone qualified is assigned to the task. It is more of a problem to keep people familiar with its content. The best way is to put it regularly to the test.

Test everything

Only by enacting 'what if' scenarios against the planned procedures and checklists will anyone become really familiar with them and know if they work. In this way, any loopholes will be discovered and may be rectified. One of the best examples of such role-playing is the 'Norox' exercise conducted each year by the UK Department of Energy. Scaled-down versions of Norox can be adapted and implemented by smaller companies to test their own response procedures.

Norox is designed to test both the operational and communications response capabilities of an operating company in the UK sector of the North Sea.

A 'what if' scenario is worked out by the Department of Energy, with the help of one or two individuals from the victim company. No-one else is privy to the scenario. The date for the exercise is kept secret until the last minute although employees of the company are notified that they are to be the subject of the exercise on an unknown day during a given month.

On the day everyone with a role to play in a real crisis enacts that role. This involves not only company employees but everyone outside the company who would become involved in a real emergency: the police, HM Coastguard, a helicopter company, the local hospital and so on. Everyone's response capabilities are tested and monitored by the Department of Energy.

The roles of relatives, friends and the media are enacted by some twenty senior public relations practitioners employed by oil companies operating in the UK sector of the North Sea. The exercise is followed by a mock press conference and detailed de-brief in which all the key players state how things went from their standpoint. At the end of it all, the Department of Energy produces a major report on the exercise which is circulated to all other operating companies in the North Sea's UK sector.

The tone of the Norox report is constructive rather than critical, along the lines of 'another time it might be better if . . .', but, after each one, there are new, positive lessons which are learnt and shared by the oil industry.

The victim company for the exercise will often spend many months preparing for Norox by reviewing and testing its procedures and carrying out mini-Norox exercises. Of course, this is one of the principal values of the whole Norox concept.

With other pressures and priorities on their time, there are few business executives who are able to keep well-versed with the thick crisis management contingency plan sitting on the shelf in their office. Familiarity with, and testing the efficiency of procedures, can only be effectively accomplished by regular rehearsal. Develop a detailed scenario, employing as few people as possible to ensure its secrecy. Check the procedures and facilities by running a full scale mock emergency based on the prepared scenario.

Have each stage of the emergency monitored by qualified observers — either qualified outside consultants or members of company management who are sufficiently qualified but would be unlikely to play a mainstream role in a real emergency.

In running rehearsals, mechanisms for making the mock incident evolve over real or imagined time need to be developed. An effective means of doing this, having developed the scenario, is to place typed details of each new phase of the scenario into a series of individual envelopes. Distribution of each envelope to the head of the crisis management team (chief executive, senior operations manager, or whoever is lead player in the rehearsal), should be timed in advance to coincide with each particular phase of the scenario. Thus, at 10.15 am the chief executive might receive an instruction reading: 'You have just learnt from the general manager of your company's manufacturing plant in Manchester that an explosion has taken place in or near the main storage depot. Several employees are unaccounted for, feared dead or injured in the wreckage. The media are onto the story. Some are arriving at the gates of the plant, many are on the telephone. The MP for Manchester is on the phone now wanting to speak to you. Take whatever action you see fit.'

He will receive a series of such messages, sometimes at intervals of only a few minutes. He will then activate his crisis management team and begin taking appropriate actions. Role-playing journalists, relatives, MPs, financial analysts and others need to be in place to test the public relations, employee relations and other communications responses of the organization. Ideally, the rehearsal should conclude with a 'live', filmed press conference attended by designated members of the crisis management team, together with the role-playing journalists.

That evening, or as soon as possible after the rehearsal, when events and actions are still fresh in peoples' minds, a detailed de-brief needs to be conducted at three levels: self-evaluation by the crisis management team, evaluation by the qualified observers, and a longer term analysis and feedback by the crisis management team at some point after the exercise.

The crisis management team usually rates itself unrealistically highly immediately after the exercise. This is to be expected because of the excitement and intensity of the simulation and the unusual nature of the experience. Whether the qualified observers are composed of company employees or an external team, this second evaluation is generally more realistic and can therefore be more constructive. Members of the crisis management team should be allocated specific tasks designed to plug any gaps in the system which are brought to light by the de-brief. Suggestions for improvement may centre on team membership, call-out procedures, further training, use of existing or new policies, tools to aid decision-making, or facility improvements.

Coping at the personal level

At a personal level, general guidelines for people coping with the crisis include:

1   Place a high priority on the morale of employees, their welfare and safety. Without it, the operation can collapse because of lack of confidence in the person in charge.

2   Be prepared to cope with an extended period under a high level of pressure and stress. So do not exceed normal levels of alcohol and cigarettes—reduce them if possible.

3   Always expect the unexpected. Be prepared to change plans as things never go as anticipated; and never underestimate the gravity of the situation. It is always safer to adopt a worst-scenario approach to

what has happened. Taking such an approach can only ensure that things get better, not worse.

4   Unorthodox methods of operation are often essential so the ability to bend the rules can prove vital.

5   Develop a wide variety of information sources. Cultivate journalists and local opinion formers. Keep up-to-date on reports on local radio, television and the press.

6   Attach no stigma to employees who want to leave when a crisis occurs. Let them go. There are enough problems to cope with without having to look after less stable staff members.

7   Communicate the situation to head office, on a regular basis, without dramatizing it. Remember that media reports which head office is receiving tend to emphasize the most threatening aspects of the situation.

Planning for crisis summarized

1   *Develop a positive attitude towards crisis management.*

2   *Bring the organization's performance into line with public expectation.*

3   *Build credibility through a succession of responsible acts.*

4   *Be prepared to act on the opportunities during a crisis.*

5   *Appoint a crisis management team.*

6 *Catalogue potential crisis situations.*

7 *Devise policies for their prevention.*

8 *Formulate strategies and tactics for dealing with each potential crisis.*

9 *Appoint crisis control and risk audit teams.*

10 *Identify who will be affected by any given crisis.*

11 *Devise effective communications channels for minimizing damage to the organization's reputation.*

12 *Put the plan in writing.*

13 *Test, test and test again.*

The object is to have all the systems tested and in place, hoping they will not be needed, but ready and able to meet a major crisis tomorrow. Crisis management can be likened to an insurance policy. It is when the reminder hasn't been paid that the fire strikes.

Bibliography and references

Donald R Stephenson, 'Converting Crisis into Cheers: deeds versus declarations', *International Public Relations Review*, August 1985.

CHAPTER 4

Surviving the Unwanted Takeover Bid

Fuelled by record share prices in the mid-1980s, merger mania resulted in the greatest takeover spree ever. It engulfed such combines as Debenhams, Dunlop, British Home Stores, Coats Paton, Imperial Group and Distillers. Companies are more vulnerable to the unexpected takeover bid than ever before. According to an *Observer* report, the value of corporate takeover bids launched in the UK during the first quarter of 1986 amounted to more than £20 billion. This compares with £3.2 billion for the first quarter of the previous year and £6.4 billion for the whole of 1985. As the takeover bids flowed, so the ripples encompassed industry, Whitehall and the City.

It is often argued that although takeovers may or may not be economically successful, the threat of takeover energizes management. The threat of takeover can produce improvements in efficiency but, equally, it can lead to the worst decisions of all. Cutting capital investment and other long-term projects in order to produce a short-term increase in profits may push up the share price and make the company that much more insulated against takeover — but at what cost over the long-term?

Nevertheless, the judiciary duty of directors of publicly quoted companies remains to their shareholders. They must watch for the tell-tale signs of an unwanted takeover looming and have plans in place for fending it off to the best of their ability.

Watching for the tell-tale signs

Planning for the unexpected when it applies to the financial aspects of a company's business (usually ownership) differs little from other corporate crises. Preparation is everything. It boils down once again to deeds versus declaration. If a company is seen to be well-managed, motivating its managers and keeping its shareholders happy, it has the best possible of takeover defences. If, however, any of these key ingredients are missing altogether, or if one of them is the weak link in the chain, then the unwanted takeover bid can be expected to present itself sooner or later.

Takeovers are about perceived values. If shareholders can be convinced that the value of their investments will be significantly increased in either the immediate or long term, they will be more likely to accept an offer, even if the management rejects it.

The tell-tale signs are all too familiar and the recent spate of major contested takeover bids has caused many companies to review their defence strategies. They include earnings that are either static or falling, a poor return on capital, an unhealthy dividend policy and bad cash management and situations where the value of the component parts of a company are worth more than the whole. A company may be too highly geared, with too little of the right investment. Its rights issues may be too frequent and poorly justified.

If a predator can spot the potentially greater value of a target's assets, it can exploit the fact that the company's management has not made full use of those assets. These may include a well-stocked pension fund; a cash mountain not earning its keep can also attract attention. Usually though, it is poor management which is the key to a company's problems — though often the last element to be identified. Frequently bids are made for companies that have set out on ventures which prove too much to handle with their available resources.

Sometimes external factors come into play which are outside the company's control, like tax, protectionism or nationalization. A major shareholder might decide to sell shares suddenly, triggering off an unforseen bid.

Neglected communications with shareholders, the investing public and the financial community in general can also prepare the ground for the unwanted bid.

But there are other reasons too, not connected with a company's poor performance; for example, business synergy. Bringing the company into the predator's fold might improve the earnings prospects of the combined companies; or possibly marketing advantages may arise if both companies involved were to make complementary products or to have complementary marketing facilities.

A bid may involve the takeover of a rival company, which might otherwise develop into a serious threat to the bidder; or the bidder may be looking for management strengthening or additional production capacity.

To fend off unwelcome predators a company has to move quickly. The odds favour the predator. Of 139 bids for UK public companies in 1985, only 28 failed.

Nevertheless, there are a number of precautions a company can take to ensure that it is better prepared to cope with an unwanted bid.

Planning against a takeover

If a bid is made, the defending company must be seen to fight fairly and fully in accordance with the Takeover Code. A rationale has to be published immediately stating convincing arguments as to why shareholders should not accept. Because the target company will probably be in a state of shock, the outline of such a statement needs to be prepared in advance and updated regularly.

83

The Takeover Code is administered by the Panel on Takeovers and Mergers and regulates all methods of obtaining control of a company. It applies to private companies which have a public element and to public companies — listed or unlisted — which are resident in the UK, Channel Islands or the Isle of Man. The Code embraces a number of general principles and rules which are interpreted by the Panel and applied in accordance with their spirit, not their letter. The main objective of the Code is to protect the interests of shareholders in a target company, for whom it aims to secure:

- Equality of treatment and opportunity.

- Adequate and equal information.

It also seeks to ensure that no frustrating action is taken by the board of the target company without its shareholders' approval, and to see that the market is conducted in an orderly fashion which serves to protect the City's reputation.

Crisis management team

A crisis management team needs to be appointed, ready to move into action at a moment's notice. Usually it will consist of the chairman or the chief executive, finance director, with perhaps a third main board director or company secretary. It will also include the head of public relations, and outside advisors from the company's merchant bank, public relations consultant and legal advisor.

Members of the crisis management team need to be relieved of all their normal day-to-day duties during the defence and must be allowed to concentrate solely on implementing the defence strategy. Other directors and executives must be seen to be getting on with running the normal operations of the company.

As with any form of corporate crisis, the communication aspects of how an unwanted takeover bid is handled will play a critical role in its success or failure.

Know your audience

To be able to convince the audience, it helps to have a fairly clear idea of who they are. A breakdown of the share register should be maintained on the basis of the size of the shareholding, whether it is a private, institutional or nominee holding, its geographical area and the average length, in time, of the shareholding. Rights under law of discovering the identity of investors behind nominee holdings should be invoked and a track kept of the broking firms actually involved in the larger share transactions.

A knowledge of the size of the shareholding and details of its type should give a good indication of where the sphere of voting influence lies. The geographical spread will give an idea as to where regional advertising might play a role. The length of time for which shares have been held will give an indication of shareholder loyalty.

If, for example, a large proportion of a company's shareholders has held shares for around five years but the share price, profits or dividend growth have fallen considerably over that same period, continued shareholder loyalty might be open to question in the event of an attractive-looking bid.

Define your message

Similarly, if a company is performing below its perceived capabilities, it needs to convey that it does indeed know where it is going. A comprehensive presentation of the company's business strategy must be produced and communicated to all those involved with the business. The shareholders, particularly the investing institutions, should be well-informed. Externally, regular meetings with stockbrokers and journalists will lead to a better appreciation of the company and fewer nasty surprises.

It is also useful to carry out regular surveys of shareholder attitudes. If a benchmark study has been undertaken, a company will be better able to gauge shareholder perceptions by repeating surveys at critical moments.

Line up the troops

Often, a company will have a reasonable idea as to the identity of a potential bidder. If this is the case, the company at the receiving end of the potential bid should check the predator's merchant bankers and stockbrokers against its own. In several recent battles it was discovered that the advisors to the two companies were the same. Valuable days will be saved in looking for new advisors if these are checked out in advance.

Key data on which a successful defence could be based needs to be regularly reviewed and updated. Included should be shareholder information, financial data per share, trading performance, forecasts and the company's business strategy.

Watch what you say

While shareholders' impressions of the company are likely to be a key factor in determining the outcome of the bid, the reputation of the company in the industry in which it operates can be as important a factor in determining whether a bid materializes. For example, if it became widely known that a company was badly managed, either generally or in one of the specialized fields such as finance, this could provide the motivation to launch a bid. For this reason, it is important that the company maintains a highly professional relationship in its dealings with other companies operating in the same industry.

Shareholders and others form their impressions about a company from meetings they may have with its representatives, from contact with other members of the financial community and from what they read in company documents, brokers' circulars and the media. All these points of contact are crucial and need to be reviewed from time to time to see if any improvements can be made.

Once a takeover bid has been announced however, no company can anticipate a smooth ride, and expectation should be that the going will get rougher. As in war, strategy is the key to either a successful takeover or a successful defence.

The battle between Arthur Bell and Guinness

Despite the rolling of various executive heads, the recent successful £356 million bid for Bell, the Scotch whisky distiller, by Guinness, the brewer, makes an interesting study when looking at strategies employed. Because it encompasses many of the points made on the previous pages, it is worth looking at this detailed account of the battle, described by Colin Chapman in his book *How the New Stock Exchange Works*.

> If one was to believe the Guinness propaganda campaign, Bell was a company less than competently run, in urgent need of salvation. The truth was a little different. Arthur Bell and Co. manufactured one of Britain's most successful and distinctive products, Bell's whisky, as well as having a

number of other useful assets. It was fiercely proud of its Scottish roots, and had enjoyed a ten-year record of unbroken growth of profits and dividends. It was, in no sense, a company needing help.

Whatever the Guinness board may have said, they knew this only too well, and therefore spent 18 months preparing themselves for a long and bitter battle.

It was not enough just to study Bell's balance sheet; Guinness needed to know all there was to know about the whisky business, for it is a ferociously competitive one, with some of the rival and best known brands, such as Johnnie Walker and Teachers, in the hands of large groups like Allied Lyons. The Monopolies Commission would not, of course, permit a bid by Allied had one even been contemplated, but Guinness had to be sure it could run Bell's at least as well as the existing owners.

Furthermore, takeover strategy these days is not confined merely to obtaining enough shares in the targeted concern. In almost every situation, politics and public relations come to the fore.

In some cases, they take precedence: for example, when United Newspapers, a medium-sized publisher of provincial newspapers with no national newspaper of its own, wanted to bid for Fleet Newspapers, publisher of the *Daily Express* and *Sunday Express*, it had first to seek the permission of the Monopolies Commission. It was even deemed impolitic to indicate a price, so Fleet shareholders had to play a guessing game for months.

This was also true with the Guinness bid for Bell. Guinness had, as its financial adviser, Morgan Grenfell merchant bank, and Cazenove and Company, the pre-eminent stock-broking experts in corporate finance, who wisely also employed another large firm of stockbrokers, Wood Mackenzie and Co., who had Scottish origins, a large industry Scottish base, and in-depth research knowledge of the whisky industry.

They quickly reported that an analysis of the Bell shareholders' register revealed that London institutional shareholders were among the main investors, and control could probably be won in the City. But Guinness also had to be able to count on political support, both in Westminster and in Scotland, where independence aspirations run strong. It therefore sought the advice of Sir Gordon Reece, the media consultant, and appointed Edinburgh's leading merchant bank, Noble Grossart, to act on its behalf, and to be ready to reassure Scottish interests when the time came for the shouting to begin.

Despite, perhaps because of, all these preparations, word emerged that someone was sniffing around at Arthur Bell and Co. and on 13 June 1985 there was a sharp rise in the Bell share price. At this point the Bell board made a fatal mistake.

The chairman, Raymond Miquel, was out of the country on a business trip to the United States. When a takeover bid appears imminent, it is essential for the captain to be on the bridge, and Miquel erred in not catching the overnight flight from Chicago to London. The next day Guinness swooped. In a short statement to the Stock Exchange it announced a £327m bid. For five days Miquel remained in Chicago, occasionally taking in telephone calls and condemning the offer.

On his return to Britain, he then made what was perhaps another mistake; he held a press conference, not in Edinburgh, but in London's Hilton Hotel, waiting until the following day to repeat the message for disgruntled but influential Scottish journalists.

Guinness, by contrast, had played it clever. The Guinness bid was timed for late Friday, always a good time for a takeover offer. Advised by Broad Street Associates, a City finanical public relations firm whose managing director, Brian Basham, had been a veteran of many successful takeovers, including the successful bid by Egyptian Al Fayed brothers for the House of Fraser, Ernest Saunders, Guinness's chief executive, devoted most of Friday evening and Saturday to briefing financial journalists and stockbroking analysts, insisting that the offer was both logical and likely to succeed. He had a receptive audience, and was rewarded with substantial favourable publicity in the Sunday newspapers. But even before he had read the results of these efforts, Saunders caught the British Airways shuttle to Edinburgh, and on Sunday was available in his hotel ready to face the probings of inquisitive Scottish journalists and brokers anxious to discover what might happen to their beloved whisky company under Guinness ownership. Saunders won several friends on that trip, and it was his frequent returns to Edinburgh as the battle intensified over succeeding weeks that played no small part in creating the atmosphere that led to a majority of Bell's shareholders accepting the offer.

While Saunders had gained the upper hand for Guinness, Bell was floundering. When the offer had been delivered to its head office in Perth, its directors discovered that the firm they thought was its merchant bank in such matters, Morgan Grenfell, was acting for Guinness. Four days later it lodged a formal complaint to the City Takeover Panel, and sought legal advice as to whether it could sue. It was a lost cause. Morgan's pointed out that it had not been asked to act for Bell for 18 months, and noted that the whisky company was also consulting another merchant bank, Henry Ansbacher. (It is not unusual for a company to have more than one merchant bank, just as individuals often maintain more than one bank account.) Bell also did not have a financial public relations firm with the expertise of Broad Street Associates at the end of a telephone, and its brokers also lacked the nous of Cazenove and Co.

It was almost one week after the bid before Bell's board was able to swing into action. A strong political supporter, Bill Walker, Tory MP for Tayside, made representations to the Office of Fair Trading that it should block the Guinness bid. The OFT rejected his advice. Miquel, back in Perth, jetted up and down to London, working on Bell's defence. Finally, on 25 June, 11 days after the bid, Bell appointed a City heavyweight, merchant bankers S G Warburg and Co., to act on its behalf.

For the Guinness team, this indicated that the struggle was far from over. Warburg's reputation as defendants on the takeover chess board was as good as Morgan Grenfell's was for attack. Guinness moved to stage two — a £1m advertising campaign in the press unlike anything seen in any previous takeover campaign. Readers of the *Financial Times*, accustomed to the drabness of tombstone advertisements, were suddenly treated each breakfast time to black headlines two inches tall. 'Bell's on the Rocks?' said one, above a telling graph comparing the company's relative share performance with the FT-Actuaries All Share Index. The Bell share price graph showed a sharp fall, and the accompanying copy said, 'Shareholders are now paying the price of the failure of Bell's management to tackle its problems. Even in its latest defence document, the board of Bell's have given no indication that it recognizes that problems exist, let alone has plans to overcome them.'

Bell's responded with its own full-page advertisements. The type size was even larger, and the language as vituperative, but the advertisements lacked the panache of those placed by Morgan Grenfell on behalf of Guinness. 'Bell's has growth potential, Bell's is a sound investment,' one advertisement proclaimed. 'Ignore the Guinness slogans. Guiness' publicity marks its basic weakness in business and management methods.'

Guinness, and its financial advisers, were not going to take this lying down. Each day Saunders and his aides met to dream up more slogans, occasionally using the 'Guinness is good for you' slogan which the company had not been permitted to use for product advertising because it could not prove its truth. In the case of financial advertising, no such proof was required.

'Will your Bell's shares ever be worth as much to you again?' asked a new advertisement, containing just one message — 'before the 262p Guinness offer, Bell's shares had stood on the market at only 143p.' A few days later this message was followed up with another, in similar vein: 'How to make your Bell's investment worth 90 per cent more.'

Meanwhile Bell's merchant bankers were doing their best to present Bell as a company with more to offer shareholders under their existing directors than under Saunders. Shortly before midnight on 5 August a second defence document was published, containing an upwardly revised profits forecast, and the pledge of a 66 per cent increase in dividend. In the document, chairman Miquel also said that its refurbished Piccadilly Hotel would soon contribute extra profits.

Once again Guinness was ready with a response. It published further advertisements claiming that Bell's share of the Scotch whisky market had declined by 20 per cent in the previous five years. It picked up five optimistic statements by Miquel, and ran what it said were 'the facts' in a second column against them.

In other words, good hard-hitting stuff. But it took real money for Guinness to clinch the deal. It increased its bid, offering Bell shareholders four new ordinary stock plus £2.65 in cash for every five ordinary shares in Bell. It also bought a 3.25 per cent stake in Bell owned by Ladbroke, the gaming and leisure group, which had earlier discussed with Bell the possibility of buying its hotels.

For the shareholders the contest was over. For them the danger had been that failure to accept the Guinness offer would almost certainly have led to the share price drifting sharply back to its earlier lower levels.

The Guinness example indicates how necessary it is for all involved in a takeover — company executives, merchant banks, stockbrokers, accountants, and public relations men — to keep on their toes. The predator in a takeover also enjoys one major advantage: it can always count on the full support of its management team, which usually has much to gain from taking charge of a larger organization. By contrast the management of a target company often finds itself in a difficult, even ambivalent, position; its loyalties are to its present board of directors, but its future, as likely as not, will lie elsewhere. It also has the burden of dealing with a worried staff, not to mention suppliers, distributors, and others with whom the company has close connections. And it has to continue to run the business.

On the other hand, experience shows that shareholders will tend to stand by a business that has done well by them, unless those making the bid make an irrefutable case. Ralph Halpern of Burton and his accomplice, Sir Terence Conran, had to fight long and hard and paid dearly for control of Debenhams, whose major shareholders, including its chairman, walked away with a tidy profit.

It is also true that the best defence against a takeover is to act before a bid, rather than afterwards — in other words, take action which will deter a predator from striking, such as selling off subsidiaries which do not fit the core of the business, or explain the company's strategy to analysts and institutions in such a way that the share price rises to reflect an accurate, rather than an undervalued, view of its stock.

Once a bid is made, it is hard to do this, because any disposals or other capital restructuring have to be approved by shareholders.

Timetable of a takeover

Companies that find themselves involved in takeovers should take note of the following timetable laid down by the Takeover Panel.

Day 0

The bidder publishes its offer document. This comes within 28 days of a firm intention to bid being announced.

Day 1

Shareholders of the target company can accept the offer from now on.

Day 14

The defence document must be posted.

Day 21

The bidder must say what acceptances have been received. If a majority of shareholders have not been won over, the company can withdraw, increase the offer, or extend the bid by periods of between seven and 14 days. Most bidders extend to a day after number 39 so they can have the last word.

Day 39

Deadline for publication of crucial evidence by the target company, including profit forecasts, proposed dividends, and general performance.

Day 42

Shareholders who have accepted the first offer made by the bidder are free to change their minds.

Day 46

Last date for raising the bid. The bidder has one more week to attack its opponent, which is unable to respond. The offer remains open for another two weeks, during which time the bidder cannot raise its stake in the target company to more than 30 per cent.

Day 60

Decision day. All acceptances must be received by 3 pm, and the announcement of success or failure has to be made by 5 pm.

Two developments can disturb this timetable. First, the intervention of another bidder. This usually leads to the Takeover Panel extending the deadlines to allow for the disruption and extra work.

Secondly, there can be a referral of the bid to the Monopolies and Mergers Commission. The Secretary of State for Trade and Industry can refer a merger at any time during the bid and in the six months after it has taken place. A merger may be investigated by the Monopolies and Mergers Commission if the two companies together supply or consume over 25 per cent of goods or services in a UK sector, or the gross value of the worldwide assets taken over exceeds £30 million or on 'national interest' grounds. On referral the bid falls although a new bid may be permitted following the MMC investigation.

Before summarizing this chapter with a checklist of the key elements required in a plan to ward off unwelcome predators successfully, mention should be made of a relatively new development, at any rate in the UK, which may present itself in a takeover situation. This is the arrival of the 'dirty tricks brigade'.

The dirty tricks brigade

For many years in America, firms of private detectives have been employed to go into every detail of the private and public lives of rival companies. There are specialist firms in New York, large and perfectly respectable, which do little else. Nonetheless, the UK financial community is disturbed to find the dirty tricks brigade beginning to manifest itself in Britain too.

During the bid by Argyll Holdings for Distillers, in 1986, it was widely reported in the press that a former employee of a James Gulliver company was approached by a man purporting to carry out 'international investigations'.

The man wanted information about Gulliver and was reported as willing to pay up to $10,000 if it was good enough to lose Gulliver, chairman of Argyll Holdings, his £2.5 billion bid for the whisky group.

The ex-Gulliver employee was aware of the significance of the approach. He recorded the conversation and sent the tape and a signed affidavit to one of Gulliver's right-hand men. James Gulliver was subsequently reported in the press as saying: 'He has information which could only have come from Distillers or their advisors. It is the dirty tricks department at work. I have been followed for days, we have been under surveillance, and we know that people have been going over every detail of my personal life going back more than thirty years.'

Distillers denied that it had ever 'been concerned with the personal or private life' of Gulliver but, later, results of the investigations surfaced. After a press conference held by Distillers to discuss its latest takeover proposals, a copy of a document was 'selectively leaked' to several newspapers by persons as yet unknown.

It showed that James Gulliver's entry in *Who's Who* was not strictly correct, and that despite a glittering academic career, he had never been a student at Harvard University — which is what the *Who's Who* entry implied.

Most City fund managers dismissed the news of Gulliver's academic record as irrelevant to the more serious issues of who has the best team to run Britain's biggest whisky company. But, according to a report in the *Sunday Times* shortly afterwards, one large investment company held a board meeting at the weekend and, according to one person there, spent some time discussing it.

'One director argued that it had nothing to do with the bid and should be ignored. But the man who actually invests the funds took a different line. He reckoned if Gulliver could be misleading about a little matter, he could be misleading about a bigger one.'

At the time, the Gulliver affair began to focus attention in Britain on the increasingly dubious tactics creeping into takeover bids. Bids have begun moving into the courts — a new development on this side of the Atlantic — and into newspapers through multi-million pound advertising campaigns. (Unfortunately for jaded readers of the financial press, these advertisements went too far for the Takeover Panel and the Financial Services Act endorses the banning of such ploys).

When dirty tricks come to light, they can read like a spy thriller. At the Birmingham brewer Davenports, fighting off a £30 million offer from Wolverhampton and Dudley, a radio transmitter was discovered taped under a boardroom table. It was powerful enough for transmission to be monitored from nearby buildings or a parked car. From the condition of its battery power pack, the device had obviously been in use for some time!

Dirty tricks aside, the following is a checklist of points to remember in your preparation against attack from an unwanted predator.

Ways to fend off unwelcome predators

1 *Pay attention to danger signals.*

- Static or falling earnings

- Poor return on capital

- Unhealthy dividend policy

- Bad cash management

- Too high gearing

- Poor investment policy

- Too many, difficult to justify, rights issues

- Unimaginative asset management (including well-stocked pension fund or cash mountain)

- Neglected communications with shareholders and the financial community in general.

2 *Look out for less obvious signals.*

- Major shareholder suddenly selling off shares

- Upcoming tax or protectionist legislation

- Business synergy with the predator (improved earnings prospects of the combined companies)

- Marketing synergy

- Knocking you out as direct competition

- Acquiring your management team

- Acquiring extra production capacity

3 *Have a crisis management plan.*

- Designation of crisis management team which includes external advisors not employed by likely predators

- Outline, updated, rationale for why shareholders should reject the bid — available for immediate publication

- Back-up statement containing clear, detailed future business strategy

- Share register breakdown: private, institutional or nominee; by geographical area and length in time of shareholding

- Quick access to financial data per share, trading performance and forecasts

4 *If cornered, know your options.*

These may include:

- Find a 'white knight'

- Look for referral opportunities to the Monopolies and Mergers Commission (as did The Royal Bank of Scotland when being stalked by the Hong Kong Bank Group)

- Organize a management buyout (as did Haden to see off an unwanted bid from Trafalgar House)

- Use the courts (something of a new defence tactic in the UK but widely used in the US).

Bibliography and references

Colin Chapman, *How the New Stock Exchange Works*, Hutchinson Business, 1986.

CHAPTER 5

Tell Your Own Tale

'The vacuum caused by a failure to communicate is soon filled with rumour, misrepresentation, drivel and poison,' said C Northcote Parkinson. The 'no comment' syndrome, especially in a crisis situation, is like a red rag to a bull. Witholding information encourages speculation and often results in an inaccurate picture of the incident building up. Worse, it can lead to accusations of a 'cover-up'. Effective management of communications is as vital as effective management of the crisis itself. After all, external perceptions about the crisis, among key audiences, will depend entirely on what they hear, see and read about it.

Horror stories about everyday products and the companies that make them are the bread and butter of the media, and there never seems to be any shortage of them. Equally, the media are filled with the intricate details of the unwanted takeover bid, companies' collapsing share prices because they have been caught napping by major changes in the consumer marketplace — remember how the Swiss watch industry failed to foresee the impact of Japanese quartz watches? Or they are filled by some calamitous disaster which claims the lives of many. When the Bhopal disaster struck, members of the news media went into immediate action. Rumours, unconfirmed reports and speculation about causes of the accident abounded, filling the airwaves while Union Carbide officials sought desperately to learn the truth. Although the company sent safety experts from the US to Bhopal immediately, it was to be nearly three months until the real causes of the accident were known. Meanwhile, the immediate need for news caused media representatives to seek information from an ever widening variety of sources.

This chapter looks at some very different examples of how the media has been handled during corporate crises and draws some lessons from those experiences. The following chapter then suggests policies and procedures for managing media communications during a crisis situation.

The Sellafield saga

Leaks at the Sellafield nuclear processing plant in the UK have been extremely damaging, if not for the radiological safety of the public and workforce, at least for the reputation of British Nuclear Fuels, operators of the plant. Individually, the incidents may well have been minor. Taken together, however, the incidents have caused considerable concern and poor communications work by BNFL meant that it failed to allay the safety fears.

One of the most serious events occurred on 5 February 1986. Plutonium mist escaped when compressed air was blown across a liquid containing plutonium. This triggered an amber alert — the first for many years — and about thirty non-essential staff had to leave the building. About forty were left behind to deal with the leak and to maintain safety in the rest of the plant.

The way BNFL dealt with the announcement of this leak shows the dilemma faced by a company in this situation. On the one hand it recognizes that it has to be as open as possible to reassure the public it has nothing to hide. On the other, information released in small chunks day after day only serves to prolong the agony. Each new piece of information gives journalists an excuse to keep the story going.

The leak started some time between 10.45 am and

11.45 am. Not surprisingly, the press was quickly tipped off that something had happened. With scores of workers rushing about, and an amber alert, it was to be expected that the news would soon get out. But, according to James Wilkinson, BBC TV Science Correspondent, when the telephone began to ring before lunchtime it was clear that the press office had not been properly briefed about what was going on. Says Wilkinson: 'All it could do was lamely promise that there would be a statement, eventually.' It was well after 4 pm when the statement did emerge, leaving a period of several hours for adrenalin levels to build up on Fleet Street.

Next, there were not enough press officers on duty to deal with the calls, and journalists found themselves waiting in a long queue. Uncertainty breeds panic, as the authorities at Three Mile Island found to their distress.

The third mistake was that BNFL seemed to have given up running the press office after normal office hours. According to Wilkinson: 'Callers ringing in the evening were told by the switchboard to leave their number for the duty press officer to ring them back.' The press office should have been fully staffed well into the night to deal with late calls from the media.

Examples such as Bhopal, Sellafield and scores of others — not least Chernobyl — demonstrate the crucial need for an effective communications strategy and action plan to be an integral part of the overall crisis contingency plan.

BNFL eventually began to get the message. They subsequently announced a £2 million advertising campaign inviting the public to 'drop in' and see the Sellafield Exhibition Centre. The open-door policy came after a year's research into consumer attitudes showed that the nuclear industry's perceived secrecy was losing it the public debate. One would hardly think it would take a year's research to conclude the obvious. Still, it was a start.

In communications terms, the immediate lessons to be

drawn from the Sellafield experience may be summarized as follows:

1 *Senior management must trust its press office and keep it up-to-date with developments as well as steps being taken to control the situation.* It then becomes the responsibility of the public relations manager, in conjunction with senior management, to exercise his or her professional judgement in deciding what information is to be disseminated to the media and how.

2 *Ensure that there are sufficient personnel within the organization trained to help cope with incoming media calls.* Few organizations can afford the luxury of maintaining a press or public relations department large enough to deal with the hundreds of media calls that will be received in the event of a crisis. Select staff who normally hold other positions of responsibility in the company and train them to assist in dealing with media calls at a time of emergency.

3 *Remember the media do not work from nine-to-five. Particularly if a major catastrophe is involved, the company will be receiving calls from all around the world, from journalists operating in different time zones. Man the press office twenty-four hours a day, if necessary.*

Toxic shock syndrome

Toxic shock syndrome, a 'disease' linked to tampon useage, made its mark on an unsuspecting world in the summer of 1980. During May of that year the American Centre of Disease Control reported an increasing incidence of a possibly fatal disease, mainly affecting menstruating women (a large proportion of the world's population!). After more research, the Centre said that

Procter and Gamble's *Rely* brand was involved in more cases than other rival lines. America's Food and Drug Administration became involved and, although no-one could conclusively prove that tampons alone triggered off TSS, Procter and Gamble decided to take *Rely* off the market fearing a possible government recall.

Procter and Gamble acted responsibly by running an advertising campaign asking women to return tampons already purchased and then giving them a refund. The American press had a field day with the situation and it wasn't long before the media in the UK began to show interest. The British press began to write stories, treating speculation as fact, citing tampon materials, plastic applicators and contaminated products as possible contributors to the disease. Whatever the connection, the disease still remains a mystery, and women had died from TSS.

At the time the UK market contained four tampon brands: *Tampax, Lilia-White's, Lil-lets*, the recently launched *Playtex*, and *Assure* for which Johnson & Johnson was carrying out a small test market. The UK industry was faced with a number of decisions and very few facts. When it was all over, Tampax's marketing director at the time, Alan Thornton, told *Marketing Week* that the company had been faced with three major decisions.

First, did the product present a hazard to consumers? Initial informed comment from most of the UK medical authorities was dismissive. The company sold, and still sells, millions of tampons each year in the UK alone and no-one was linking tampon usage to TSS. This suggested that the industry was not responsible for the 'epidemic', as some of the more sensational press reports implied.

Secondly, Tampax had to decide whether to cut back on advertising and lie low until the situation resolved itself — but would it? Even then to axe promotional expenditure would hint that there was something to hide, so Tampax increased its advertising expenditure.

Third was the problem of how to deal with the media. Tampax expected to be inundated with calls. When they did come, it was interesting to note the different approaches between the newspapers and womens' magazines. In the event, the company received more calls from the press than consumers.

Thornton says the dailies wanted news — sensational, overstated, dramatic headlines. He noted that anything to do with the reproductive process made great copy — witness the continuing saga of problems associated with use of the pill. In contrast, the womens' magazines and womens' page editors had a totally different emphasis. They wanted information, not sensational headlines.

The fact that much of the news was breaking in America caused problems. National newspapers were picking up juicy details on the wire services after UK office hours. Thornton says a keen journalist would then phone America and get comment from the American viewpoint but would write the story from a British angle.

The company decided that all media enquiries would be handled by one person at senior level while the switchboard and all staff likely to receive calls were briefed accordingly. Press enquiries were given absolute priority — internal meetings of whatever importance were interrupted, and when senior management were out of the building the office had a complete schedule of where they could be contacted. This meant that all questions could be answered directly and without seeming evasive. Often, says Thornton, the questions were loaded — by implication companies marketing tampons were guilty of something or other until they could prove themselves innocent. In Thornton's view it was important to put leading questions in perspective before answering them directly. A simple 'yes' or 'no' could give the wrong impression.

The two major brands in the market, Tampax and Lil-lets emerged from the situation virtually unscathed. Playtex, which had just come onto the market that year, was not so lucky. An article in the *New Statesman* falsely accused Playtex of being the product that had caused all the problems in America. The rumour was proliferated by other journalists who picked up the *New Statesman* story and suddenly Playtex was in the centre of the controversy. Resultant bad publicity and action groups formed by irate women eventually led to many stores delisting the product. Then, IPC banned Playtex's advertising. Playtex abandoned the British market.

The UK market remained virtually unaffected by the scare — if women changed their method of protection it was usually for reasons other than TSS.

Both incidents, Sellafield, and the tampon example—although widely different in scale and nature, demonstrate that journalists, constantly looking for good stories, naturally seek out news makers when crisis strikes.

More lessons come from these examples.

4   *Don't 'lie low' if you have nothing to hide.* Reducing promotional expenditure, cutting back on 'normal' media relations activity, will almost certainly serve to indicate that there is something to hide. BNFL eventually adopted an 'open door' policy; Tampax actually increased promotional activity.

5   *If guilty of some misdemeanor, go public with the facts as soon as you are sure of them and have positive plans for rectifying the situation.* You must establish yourself as the authoritative source of information about what has gone wrong because the truth will come out eventually. To be 'found out' will do untold damage to your corporate credibility.

6   *If wrongly accused of a misdemeanor, leave no stone unturned in proving the accusation to be false.* Employ unbiased, authoritative bodies to support your case;

threaten libel action unless a prominent retraction and apology is carried by the offending publication.

If corporate executives fail to provide good stories, journalists will certainly turn to others for their information. A statement, a good quote, whenever one is asked for, is often sufficient to satisfy the media. When Union Carbide officials received news about the Bhopal catastrophe, they were viewed immediately as the villains. This image was sharpened as the company scrambled desperately to gather information, putting off reporters as the pressure mounted.

The key to managing communications in a crisis is for the organization at the centre of the crisis to establish itself quickly and firmly as the authoritative source of information. It must obviously be willing and able to cooperate with the media and other external groups from the outset.

Union Carbide eventually took the initiative when the chairman, Warren Anderson, travelled to India. In itself, this was newsworthy but his arrest in India, along with two Indian executives, made headlines and resulted in some expressions of sympathy for Anderson. Subsequent announcements by the corporation — that disaster aid was being made available, that the Bhopal factory would not be reopened in absence of Indian approval and that they would close their Institute, West Virginia, plant — helped give the corporation some control over the news.

There are many ways to make news when a crisis arises. The first, and most obvious, is to provide complete information to the media, political leaders, employees, the local community, customers, shareholders, journalists and others who are likely to be interested, in anticipation of their questions. (In this context, it is interesting to note Professor Kuechle's observation that, for most of the time, companies go about their businesses in a routine way, turning out products and delivering services as a matter of course. Consequently, their activities are generally not newsworthy, and most corporate executives do not develop skills in the act of making news. By contrast, political leaders and members of special interest groups are generally well-trained in this art and they respond enthusiastically when there are opportunities for them to be heard.)

Bad day at Bantry Bay

Union Carbide's early response activities remind me clearly of my own first involvement in dealing with the media and other external groups in a crisis situation. Although not of the same magnitude, some of the problems we faced were equally tragic and complex. In the 1970s I was Gulf Oil Corporation's public affairs manager in Europe when an oil tanker, *Betelguese* belonging to Total, blew up at Gulf's terminal in Bantry Bay, Southern Ireland. The explosion killed everyone on board the tanker, and some of Gulf's own employees — fifty in all.

Direct experience in handling aspects of this tragedy taught me two key lessons: first, the need for a crisis contingency plan (we didn't have one) and, secondly, the need for companies to be conscious of the *credibility* of their actions.

Bantry Bay was selected by Gulf as a much-needed deep water port where it could transfer oil, shipped from the Middle East by very large crude carriers, too large to enter conventional European ports, onto smaller vessels which would then bring the oil to Gulf's European refineries. Opened in 1968, the Bantry Bay terminal had a good record for a number of years until, in October 1974, some 2,500 tons of oil were spilled into the Bay, followed by a further spillage of 1,100 tons in January 1975. Although not major disasters in themselves, these two spills were to have a critical impact on the credibility of statements made by the Corporation when the real disaster happened on the night of 8 January 1979.

After each spill, the terminal's general manager, under intense pressure from the local media, *speculated* about the amount of oil that had been spilled — at a time when he could have no way of knowing. On each occasion, a guess was made which turned out to be ridiculously low but the figures were widely published in the press. The next day, when the true quantities became known, the media accused the manager of attempting a cover-up, and said so loudly in their columns. Gulf's credibility with the media was shot to pieces and despite numerous press relations and local community exercises afterwards to restore this credibility, it was still poor when the big January 1979 disaster occurred.

By midnight on 7 January, two thirds of the oil had been offloaded from the *Betelguese*. Sometime around 1 am, a massive explosion took place on board, ripping the tanker in two and turning it literally into a blazing inferno. To minimize pollution, the fire was allowed to burn, and eventually, 19 hours later, it went out.

Twenty-four hours later, the stern section had sunk and the bow section, which remained afloat containing oil, posed a continuing pollution risk. Work began immediately on the recovery of the dead, and on mop-up and salvage operations.

At around 2 am on the night of the disaster, Gulf's public relations consultant, John McMahon, miles away in Dublin, was informed of the disaster in the briefest detail, and immediately began to receive phone calls from the media. He then called me at my home in the UK before he set off by car to Bantry — a drive of some five hours. By 3.30 am that morning I was on my way to Northolt Aerodrome outside London to catch a chartered plane to Bantry. Accompanying me were two senior vice-presidents from Gulf and a corporate lawyer.

News had travelled so fast among the media about the incident that it was almost impossible to charter a plane, because so many had already been chartered ahead by journalists.

Figure 5.1: Aftermath of the tragedy at Bantry Bay, Republic of Ireland.

While on my way to Ireland, the regional public relations director, Peter Hamilton, went straight to Gulf's London office where he received the first media enquiry at 4.30 am — from the BBC's Radio 4 *Today* programme. His role was to 'seize the initiative' by preparing as detailed a background press statement as possible, giving the complete history of Bantry Bay. By making the release as comprehensive as possible, it cut out endless phone calls from the media as to why the terminal had been built at Bantry, what its purpose was, and so on. By 8 am, the Irish public relations executive was at the scene, having driven from Dublin. He assembled as many known facts as possible and then phoned them through to London. By 9 am, London was able to issue its first statement, specifically about the accident, to the press.

The public relations director then assembled a team of telephonists to assist in answering media calls, which they continued to do for the next two days. The London office was able to release information, which was constantly updated by the public relations team on the spot in Ireland. In this case, London had to issue all the information because it was not possible physically or technically to do so from Bantry. Another crucial function London played was to monitor TV and radio newscasts and early press reports and to correct, or to stop at once, any rumours or misinformation that might be contained in them.

By 8.30 am, an incident room had been set up at Bantry. Gulf maintained only a very small office in the town so the meeting room of a neighbouring hotel was hired for the purpose. The Irish public relations consultant made a quick appraisal trip out to the site of the disaster and on his return, issued a short statement, via the one open phone to London, announcing a first press conference for 5 pm that day.

The Irish Premier arrived unexpectedly in Bantry and was taken out to the vessel so that he could assess for himself that Gulf was taking every reasonable step to control matters.

Meanwhile, I had landed at Cork Airport during the morning and my party was assaulted by a battery of TV crews who had somehow discovered that we were on our way. We were in no position to make any statement whatsoever. By the time I got to Bantry, within 12 hours of the disaster, there were about 80 national and international journalists already there, besieging the hotel and Gulf's office. Some had chartered planes to fly around the wreck. A stop had to be put to that, because of the risk of mid-air collisions.

We held a morning and evening press conference for the next few days. As media interest began to wane, the number was reduced to one per day. The last conference was held ten days later. All day long, calls were received from the press around the world. Because of Total's involvement, a large number of calls were received from France. Calls from radio stations often began: 'This is so and so from Radio Station X. This phone call is being tape recorded for future broadcasting. How was the explosion caused?' The public relations team's role was to answer all these press enquiries; continuously to prepare updated statements as new facts became known; to monitor press coverage for inaccuracies which had to be put right; and to brief management prior to each press conference.

The reason that news of the disaster had spread so quickly was that a senior journalist from the *Irish Times* had a holiday cottage in Bantry. One of his hobbies was to watch the ships in the bay through his binoculars and before turning in, had taken one last look at the *Betelguese*. He literally saw it blow up before his very eyes. You might think it was an exceptional set of circumstances and, of course, it was. But there is always an exceptional set of circumstances that will send news of a disaster flying around the world. He was in contact with his Dublin office in three minutes and from there the *Irish Times* was on to the wire services with its scoop. News of the disaster was being flashed around the world literally within ten minutes of it taking place. Of course, a number of other people, who were also still up and about, saw the explosion and this led inevitably to different accounts as to the time the explosion took place. Keeping in mind Gulf's credibility gap with the local media this question of timing was to become a crucial factor in later press reports.

A number of witnesses, including two policemen, told reporters that the explosion had taken place well before the time that Gulf had said it had: the implication being that Gulf had tried to contain the fire itself before calling local emergency services, spent valuable time trying to contain the fire, had failed to do so, and only then had called in the emergency services. The further implications were that lives, possibly, could have been saved had Gulf called in the emergency services immediately. In fact, as we now know, the explosion and fire were so ferocious and fast that nothing could have saved the crew or jetty personnel.

Just as this question of timing was becoming a crucial issue at press conferences, so was another, even more important issue coming into play. In Gulf's control room at the terminal, the operator, a local man from Bantry, was one of the few sole survivors of the holocaust. It was his job to press the button that would have summoned the local emergency services. The press wanted to know, 'Did he or didn't he [press the button] immediately?' Within 24 hours of the first press conference, the press were clamouring to have either the operator attend a press conference in person so he could be questioned, or to have a signed statement read out on his behalf. For legal reasons (the proposed statement could have prejudiced subsequent official enquiries), we were neither able to produce him or his statement. 'Cover-up', screamed the local press and continued to do so for three days. This was the biggest local news story

Figure 5.2: The Bantry Bay tragedy from the front page of the Cork Examiner, *January 11, 1979. The Cork Examiner established 1841 is the oldest daily newspaper in the Irish Republic.*

they'd had in years and they were going to make the most of it.

Many of the press discovered where the operator's house was and went along pretending to be gas meter readers, electricity board officials, and so on. His wife, a woman of great resilience, was able to keep them all at bay. Nonetheless, during that two to three day period, the hostility shown by the media towards Gulf at, and outside, the press conferences escalated to an unbelievable level. So much so, that it became very difficult for me to persuade senior Gulf people to attend the press conferences at all. Eventually, however, Gulf was able to defuse the situation, without producing the operator, by fielding technical staff at the conferences who could report on the progress being made on the salvage and pollution clean-up operation. *In other words, we began making our own news.*

Looking back on the press coverage, largely because of the comprehensive nature of that first release, the international media treated the disaster in much the same way as they would treat a major airline disaster: headline news for the first day and then short, follow-up stories over the next few days. The serious Sunday Press, of course, did their in-depth explanations of how they thought the explosion could have taken place. Some local magazines and TV programmes tried to do follow-up stories based on 'local feeling' towards Gulf, or ran quotes such as 'Gulf Get Out, say local inhabitants'. Fortunately, however, Gulf's work among the local community over the years had done its job of creating a bank of goodwill among inhabitants and very few said they thought Gulf was to blame.

But it must be recorded that it was the company's lack of credibility with the local media, created by the previous two unrelated incidents that continued to fuel hostile press coverage. The local Irish press kept on and on writing about the incident for at least another two or three months. To sum up, the three most valuable lessons

I learned from Bantry Bay, and which we can add to our list, were as follows:

7 *When short on facts about the crisis, make your own news to fill the void until accurate information about the incident is available for dissemination.* The early hours or days of an incident are always the most difficult to cope with because so little real information is available. Whenever possible, fill the void by issuing background information about the company, and the installation involved, to demonstrate that you are willing to cooperate and communicate with the outside world. Doing so will establish you quickly, and vitally, as the single authoritative source of information about what has gone wrong.

8 *Never fill the void with speculation or blatant untruths.* Either will haunt you for the rest of your corporate life. They may land you in court.

9 *Ensure that the organization has a list of responsible deeds and actions behind it to support the credibility of statements and claims made during the crisis situation.* These are your insurance policy for seeing that statements made and actions taken in crisis are more readily believable at a time when they most need to be.

With any crisis, the press coverage pattern tends to be roughly the same. It will be big news nationally and internationally for the first few days, but local coverage will continue for much longer. As well as the media and public, other sectors of society watch with varying degrees of interest and alarm when an emergency arises. If the company at the centre of the crisis is *seen* to operate professionally under pressure, keeping interested parties informed, it can only help to safeguard its reputation. By stating what has occurred and outlining the steps being taken to remedy the problem, it is more likely that the company will be viewed positively and even sympathetically, as was illustrated by the Tylenol example. Having in place workable procedures can reduce damaging speculative comment and will establish the company as *the* authoritative source of information.

It is important to remember, however, that the largest, and often most influential audience consists of readers, viewers and listeners who are generally reluctant to immerse themselves in details, to examine all available facts and arrive at independent conclusions about events in the news. As Professor David Kuechle has pointed out in his excellent article, 'Crisis Management: an executive quagmire', these are people who respond to images more than facts, who appreciate brevity rather than thoroughness, and to whom perceptions are often more important than reality.

Journalists who address this audience write stories which are brief, devoid of technical detail and, ideally, have emotional appeal. They know that impressions are formed during brief television appearances, by newspaper headlines and by magazines with lots of pictures. Most corporate executives are understandably reluctant to engage in exchanges with members of the media or representatives of interest groups. Yet, by preparing 15-second statements which focus on commonly shared emotions they can do a great deal to enhance the image of their organization.

The Union Carbide chairman, Warren Anderson, struck a common chord when he said, after being released by Indian officials: 'My immediate concern is to get the people affected immediate disaster relief'. He didn't once mention his Indian prison experience.

As companies become increasingly accountable for their actions to the outside world, executives can no longer afford to shirk the responsibility of communicating beyond the immediate concerns of their organization. Those that do, do so at their peril. Most executives are notoriously bad at getting their message across (a failure on the part of business schools?) An executive was being interviewed on the BBC's *Panorama* programme when he was asked how his company could go on marketing a product that had such a high health risk. This was arguably an unfair question, but he refused to answer claiming that it had not been on the list of questions submitted before the interview. Worst still, a voice off-camera (probably the public relations man) insisted that the recording should be stopped and the unfortunate incident be edited out.

Again, most of us will remember the then Secretary of State for Defence, John Nott, walking out of a television interview with Sir Robin Day after the Falklands War — it is unusual to see a politician not coping with the rigours of an interview.

In today's corporate environment, executives must be trained to get their message across as well as get themselves out of awkward spots without losing face or their composure.

Effective management of communications isn't just about dealing with the media. Different audiences require different handling. Effective crisis management often involves pro-active communication with politicians, pressure groups, employees, relatives, and the financial community. Although each group may require to be handled in a different way, what is important is that a consistency of message runs through each statement made to each group. Distraught relatives may be hearing one thing on radio broadcasts and being told something completely different by the company's employee relations department. A shareholder may be hearing one story from his professional advisor and another from the company in which he has invested. Part of the art of communications management is to ensure, as far as possible, that everyone sings from the same hymn sheet. The communications management plan must identify all parts of the organization that are likely to be contacted by different sectors of the outside world and ensure that they are kept up-to-speed with the latest authorized information.

Similarly, it is vital to identify groups external to the organization who will be involved in the crisis and who therefore will be contacted for their views by the media. Such groups might include the police, fire services, local hospitals, merchant bankers, and brokers.

By having the mechanism in place to keep all parts of the organization, and involved external groups, updated with regular, authorized information about the incident, there is a greater chance of potential adversary groups simultaneously gaining the same facts and impressions of the incident in a controlled, consistent manner. The following chapter looks at how this can be done.

Initial points to consider in developing a crisis communications plan

1 *Senior management must trust its press office and keep it up-to-date with developments, especially steps being taken to control the situation.*

2 *Ensure that there are sufficient personnel within the organization trained to help cope with incoming media calls.*

3 *Remember the media do not work from nine-to-five. Particularly if a major catastrophe is involved, the company will be receiving calls from all around the world, from journalists operating in different time zones. Man the press office twenty-four hours a day, if necessary.*

4 *Don't 'lie low' if you have nothing to hide.*

5 *If guilty of some misdemeanor, go 'public' with the*

facts as soon as you are sure of them and have positive plans for rectifying the situation.

6 *If wrongly accused of a misdemeanor, leave no stone unturned in proving the accusation to be false.*

7 *When short on facts about the crisis, make your own news to fill the void until accurate information about the incident is available for dissemination.*

8 *Never fill the void with speculation or blatant untruths.*

9 *Ensure that the organization has a list of responsible deeds and actions behind it to support the credibility of statements and claims made during the crisis situation.*

Bibliography and references

James Wilkinson, *The Listener*, February 1986.

'How to triumph over disasters', *Marketing Week*, 30 March 1984.

Professor David Kuechle, 'Crisis Management: an executive quagmire', *Business Quarterly*, Spring 1985.

Tim Traverse-Healy, 'Bantry Bay: A Case History in Crisis Management', *International Public Relations Review*, February 1986.

CHAPTER 6

Tell It All, Tell It Fast

The news media provide a cascade of information about disasters that affect companies and other organizations. Journalists are quick to pounce at such times, hungry to obtain and disseminate news. They reach so many people so quickly that their impact on public attitudes toward a company or its products can be deep and lasting. The era when a Vanderbilt could say, 'The public be dammed' is gone. Today a company's health requires a good relationship with various sectors of the public — its customers, its neighbours, its employees, its stockholders and its suppliers. And the way in which a company interacts with the media when bad news breaks is increasingly crucial to these relationships.

All too often, when bad news does break, the resulting corporate image contains negative factors. This may frequently result from a misinterpretation of events by the media, but whatever the cause, a retrospective look at the company's news-handling process in such cases usually indicates questionable judgement and inadequate preparation. No organization can afford to fail in this respect. The public is most likely to gain a bad impression if it perceives the organization to be unresponsive, confused, inept, reluctant or unable to provide reliable information.

Just as crisis can be anticipated and planned for, however, so can the organization's *response* be anticipated and planned for. This is the essence of crisis communications planning.

Why have crisis communications planning? Because the consequences of not planning are damaging to employees, to profits, to morale and to every other aspect of the organization. The consequences of any unplanned-for occurrence, however calamitous, can always be less costly and less traumatic when crisis communications are thoroughly planned in advance. And when the unexpected happens, be sure to apply the cardinal rule of crisis communications: *tell it all and tell it fast.*

Journalists will be under fierce pressure to file their stories during a crisis. If *you* don't feed them the information they need, or you don't feed it swiftly enough, they will look for other sources, which may be less knowledgeable and reliable, but which will offer them their livelihood: a story.

The best antidote, in the end, is consistent and persistent communication — day in, day out, year in, year out. This is especially true in a highly technical industry: a nuclear alert or an environmental pollution episode are examples. This is because the 'fear factor' is minimized when the general public and the news media have been well informed: they will be less prone to over-react or to panic when a crisis occurs. With consistent communication and thoughtful planning, companies are better prepared to encounter crisis with a measure of calm and emerge with a measure of success.

Identify the media

As we have already seen, a key ingredient in the planning stages of crisis management is the identification of those groups likely to be impacted by each different set of crisis circumstances. The same rule applies to the media. Draw up lists of newspapers, trade publications, wire services, radio and television stations that are likely to cover any given crisis. Such lists, complete with addresses, telephone numbers, editors' and reporters' names, can spare the firefighters endless irritation and inadvertent blunders. It shouldn't be necessary to look up telephone numbers when caught in the maelstrom of a crisis.

Don't forget that relationships you may have forged with individual reporters over several years are unlikely to be of much help in a crisis situation, because those relationships will have been developed with specialist correspondents who cover the industry in which you operate. When crisis breaks, you will be beseiged by calls from news reporters who don't know you, your company or your industry. It will be then that the *corporate* reputation of your organization for good communication (or otherwise) will be of paramount importance.

Background information to seize the initiative

It is essential to keep updated background information packs about the organization and each installation or part of the operation considered potentially at risk, together with black-and-white photographs, diagrams and any other material which can help the lay reporter to understand and communicate the nature of your business accurately. Having such packs located both at the organization's headquarters and at each installation at risk, where the press might descend in droves, will help you to seize the initiative, demonstrate your commitment to cooperating with the media, and give valuable breathing space to pull together the first detailed statement about what has gone wrong.

'The first twenty-four hours are critical', says Donald R Stephenson, director of public issues for Dow Chemical Canada Inc: 'If you aren't geared up and ready to inform the public', he adds, 'you will be judged guilty until proven innocent.'

Nevertheless, a company's first instinct is often to remain silent. The reasons are many: concern over liability, uncertainty over who should speak, sometimes confusion over what really happened.

Dow Chemical Canada decided to improve its crisis communications plans after a railway truck carrying a Dow chemical was derailed near Toronto in 1977, forcing the evacuation of 250,000 residents. Since then, Dow Canada has prepared information kits on the hazards of its products and trained executives in interview techniques.

This foresight was rewarded in 1982. Another accident spilled toxic chemicals into a river that supplied water for several towns. Almost immediately, Dow Canada's emergency-response team arrived at the site and set up a press centre to distribute information about the chemicals. It also recruited a neutral expert — the regional public health officer — to speak about the hazards and how to deal with them. The result: officials praised Dow's response.

Set up a press centre

A crucial part of Dow's response was to set up a press centre. Should a crisis occur, where would you establish a communications control centre? How and with whom would you staff it? How would you arrange for the necessary communications and office equipment? All these details, and more, can and should be planned in advance to avoid wasting precious time and energy on housekeeping details. Pre-planning the location of an emergency press centre helps to demonstrate to the media that they are not going to be fobbed off by the organization at the centre of the crisis. And it can be enormously beneficial to the organization in 'coralling' media representatives away from the actual site of the disaster — provided that they are communicated with at the centre on a regular basis.

Reconnaissance work needs to be done near each site considered at risk and arrangements made, perhaps with a local hotel, or with a town or village hall, which could be quickly established as a centre for the press during

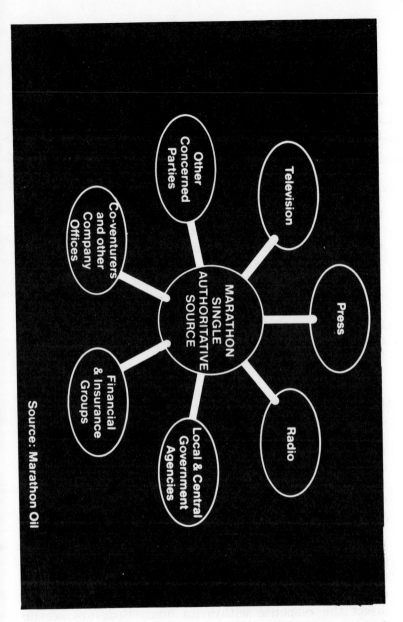

Source: Marathon Oil

Figure 6.1: Interfaces between an organization and external groups with which it will need to communicate in a time of a crisis.

an emergency. It may also be prudent to come to an arrangement with the management of the selected centre to ensure that it is equipped with sufficient power points for outside broadcasting units, and with enough telephone points, telex and facsimile machines to enable journalists to relay their stories back to their editorial offices.

The UK oil industry, centred on Aberdeen in Scotland, has come to just such an arrangement with the Grampian Regional Council. The Council has allocated designated rooms at its headquarters in the middle of Aberdeen for use by the media during an offshore emergency. Member companies of the oil industry have paid for additional telephone lines and other communications facilities which are permanently stored at the Council headquarters. A large room is capable of being transformed instantly for press conference purposes, and media representatives know that a central point exists for gathering updated information.

Emergency press centre for media calls

As well as having a central point at which media representatives can gather, the organization needs its own emergency press centre to take incoming media calls. This needs to be sited close to the emergency control centre, or 'war room', to facilitate passage of information from one to the other.

Few companies have more elaborate preparations than United Airlines Inc. Members of its crisis management team carry bleepers and are always on call. If United's Chicago headquarters receives word that a plane has crashed, for example, they can be in the 'war room' to direct the response within an hour. Beds are set up nearby so participants can catch a brief sleep from time to time; while they sleep, alternates take their places.

The job of eliciting information from the emergency

control centre for dissemination to the media and other interested parties is often the most difficult one facing the public relations manager. In the heat of the moment, the emergency control centre becomes a hubbub of decision-taking. Members of the crisis management team are too busy dealing with the operational response to the incident to take time out to brief the public relations manager. It is therefore vital that the organization's senior public relations representative is an integral member of the crisis management team, physically located, for the most part, in the emergency control centre.

If the crisis management team has been properly organized, one of its members will have been delegated to write up on boards in the centre each detail of the incident and each decision that has been taken.

Only by being located in the centre can the senior public relations representative keep abreast of fast moving developments by reading the boards, listening and contributing to the decision-taking process, and to use his or her professional judgement in deciding which elements of the unfolding crisis are ready to be committed to press releases and subsequent distribution.

Quiet room

In turn, the senior public relations representative needs at least one trained assistant who can be briefed with the latest releaseable information and turn it into a news release.

The writing of press releases needs to be done away from the noisy emergency control centre, in a room where there is sufficient peace and quiet to collate the facts and present them in the most appropriate manner. Many organizations, such as British Airways, Marathon Oil and Total Oil Marine, employ the use of a 'quiet room'. This is located next to the emergency control centre and partitioned from it by glass. Located in the quiet room are the crisis management team leader and the press release writer. By looking through the glass partition watching the information going up on the boards, and listening into conversations in the centre using an intercom, the crisis management team leader can keep abreast of the latest details, but also be in a position to think strategically about the decisions being taken and their implications. (In a simulated exercise using this system, the crisis management team handled all aspects of the operational response to the disaster with textbook precision — with one exception. In its euphoria the team omitted to send down a diving bell to rescue two trapped divers on the ocean floor who were not part of the main catastrophe. It was the team leader, sitting in the quiet room, who spotted the ghastly error and 'saved' the lives of the unfortunate divers.)

A secondary advantage of locating the crisis management team leader in the quiet room is that he can make or take telephone calls to and from key VIPs; perhaps the prime minister, a minister of state or the chairman of the board.

The press release

By also being located in the quiet room, the press release writer has access to the information on the board, enabling him to draft press releases on a rolling basis as new information becomes available. Once each new press release has been completed he has ready access to the crisis management team leader who needs to approve its final content and release.

In my view, based on my own experience of these situations, it is vital that press releases receive final approval from someone in authority where the disaster is being tackled. Sending releases through to head office, for approval by senior management remote from what is actually taking place, can add hours to distribution time and, very often, reduces the amount of information contained in the statement. It is important, of course, that someone in authority is located at the site of the crisis or can be got there quickly. And, at the risk of enraging the legal profession, my own advice is also to keep press releases well away from lawyers. They are not trained to write for the media and the necessarily restraining mentality of their profession quickly turns a helpful, informative statement into meaningless jargon. Discuss points with them by all means, but don't let them tamper with the words.

As part of the preparation process, it is often possible to have a draft crisis press release ready for distribution soon after disaster has struck. The opening paragraph can be prepared, leaving the obvious gaps to be filled in, while the remainder of the release can be prepared to contain background information on the company, and the part of the organization where things have gone wrong. For example:

PRESS RELEASE

Regester Chemicals (UK) confirms that an incident (state nature of incident if possible, eg fire) occurred at its Cardiff processing plant at approximately (insert time) today.

At this stage, specific information about any casualties or damage is not known but a detailed press statement will be issued as soon as this information becomes available. This is anticipated within (insert time).

Further press information will also be available by telephoning the following numbers (insert telephone numbers) and asking for the Press Centre.

Background information

Regester Chemicals (UK), formed in 1962, owns and operate two plants in the United Kingdom, one at Southampton and one at Cardiff. The Cardiff plant, which employs (insert number of employees) manufactures. . . .

- Describe purpose of plant

- Benefits of its products

- Safety record

- Background to owning company

If the incident is of such magnitude that it is obviously not going to go unnoticed, don't wait for the press to start calling before you issue the statement. On the other hand, there is no reason to go bursting into print if the incident is quickly and efficiently contained (without injury, with minimum damage and no further risk to employees or external groups). Nonetheless, it's always useful to have a pre-prepared release in case news leaks out.

Follow up this first release with as detailed a statement as possible containing *known* facts about what has gone wrong. Express regret and concern for what has happened, state what is being done to remedy the situation and, if appropriate, the independent bodies with whom you are cooperating, to add credibility to the actions being taken.

Keep up the flow of statements whenever there is more factual information available, and announce the time and location of a press conference if it quickly becomes apparent that one will be needed. Announcing the time of a press conference (provided that it is sensitive to newspaper deadlines) can take much of the immediate pressure off the organization, giving it time to prepare as comprehensively as possible for the conference itself. More about press conferences in a moment.

Distribution of the press release

Even if you have succeeded quickly in establishing yourself as the sole authoritative source of information about what has gone wrong, the media will still turn to other sources for information, perhaps to get a different slant, or to check on activities of others involved over which you have no control, eg the police. The important thing is to ensure, as far as possible, that you have worked out who those other groups might be and that they are at least in a position to be supportive to the actions you are taking. The only way such groups can help is if they are themselves kept aware of what you are communicating to the media.

You need, therefore, to identify these groups well in advance and send them copies of your press statements (not for approval, for information) *before* you send them to the media. Then at least you will help to ensure that the media hear the same from all affected parties, and the flow of information about what has happened is well managed.

As far as possible, everyone involved in a crisis needs to tell the same story. In communications terms, the worst problems are caused by conflicting or seemingly conflicting reports, generated from over-zealous media reporting coupled with the journalists' lack of knowledge. Some confusion is inevitable but there is no reason to contribute to it.

Once it has been approved, don't forget to let other members of the organization who may be talking to the outside world have copies of the press release. Lawyers may be talking to the police, and employee relations people talking to relatives. Everyone needs to know the latest official position to keep the risk of confusion to an acceptable minimum.

The switchboard

If it all goes wrong at the switchboard, it all goes wrong forever. Switchboard operators must be briefed and trained to know who will call the organization in a crisis situation and to whom those calls must be routed.

Switchboard guidelines should include such instructions as:

- As far as possible, the switchboard personnel should ascertain the nature of a call to a manager who may be involved with an incident. If possible they should *not* volunteer the information that an incident has taken place.

- If the manager asked for is involved in the Emergency Control Centre and the call is not of direct application to the incident, the call should be put through to the manager's secretary or an available secretary in the relevant department.

- Callers from the media and the general public should be put through to the Press Centre (or to re-dial on pre-arranged numbers depending on the system which has been put into place).

- Relatives should be dealt with sympathetically and transferred to Employee Relations.

The most critical role the switchboard operator may have to face is in the taking of a terrorist threat when the antagonist is not prepared to be transferred to someone in greater authority. The preparation of forms like the one illustrated can help to provide vital clues.

Date: .... Time Call Received: ......

Bomb Threat   Name: .... Position: .... Tel Ext: ......
Received by: Home Address: .... Tel No: ......
Exact Words
of Caller: ....
                ....
                ....
                ....
                ....

Questions   1. When is the bomb going to detonate? ....
to ask   2. Where is the bomb right now?   ....
Caller: 3. What kind of bomb is it?   ....
           4. What will cause it to go off?   ....
           5. What does it look like?   ....
           6. Why did you place the bomb?   ....
           7. Where are you calling from?   ....

The following information requires opinions, perception and judgement.
Please give your FIRST impression. (Please tick)

Caller was: ☐ Male   ☐ Adult   ☐ Female   ☐ Adult
                     ☐ Child   ☐ Child

Estimated ☐ Pre Teens ☐ Teenager ☐ 20-40 ☐ 40-50 ☐ Over 50
Age:

Caller's   ☐ Accent   ☐ Pronounced ☐ Slight ☐ Local
Speech: ☐ Irish   ☐ Scots   ☐ European ☐ Other ....

Caller's   ☐ Calm   ☐ Loud   ☐ Stutter ☐ Disguised
Voice: ☐ Angry   ☐ Normal   ☐ High   ☐ Familiar
           ☐ Slow   ☐ Distinct ☐ Deep   If familiar who did
                                    it sound like?
           ☐ Soft   ☐ Slurred   ☐ Excited ....
                                          ....

Background ☐ Street Noise ☐ T.V.   ☐ Clear   ☐ Aeroplane
Noises: ☐ Voices   ☐ House Noise ☐ Static   ☐ Train
          ☐ PA System ☐ Motors   ☐ Local   ☐ Other
          ☐ Music   ☐ Machinery ☐ Long Distance ....
          ☐ Radio   ☐ Animals ☐ Phone Box ....

Threat   ☐ Well Spoken ☐ Foul   ☐ Incoherent ☐ Taped
Language:

Remarks: ....
              ....
              ....

                      Signature:............................

Figure 6.2: A bomb threat questionnaire for switchboard operators.

The press conference

Calling a press conference to announce the tragic outcome of a terrible accident is a very different matter from holding a conference to show off the latest model from your car range. The chances are that you will have come straight from dealing with the problem in the emergency control centre. You will be in an agitated frame of mind, and may have already gone for many hours without sleep. But never, ever allow yourself to be bamboozled into walking in front of a potentially hostile press audience without being prepared. Many have done it before you and lived to rue the day. Nonetheless, there are many good reasons for holding press conferences in crisis situations:

- First, the press may have gathered at the scene of the disaster or outside the company's headquarters, demanding more information and interviews where they can put questions.

- Secondly, holding a press conference provides an ideal opportunity for the company to recap on the events of the previous few hours and ensure that the media truly understand what has happened and what steps have been taken to remedy the situation.

- Thirdly, it provides the organization with a forum where it can express concern and regret for what has happened by putting human faces to words which hitherto have only been expressed down the telephone or on paper.

- Fourthly, it enables television and radio to obtain what is termed 'actuality' — filmed footage or taped sound for use in broadcast news bulletins. (This is always preferable to a news reporter talking into a microphone on the front steps of your building.)

- Fifthly, and most importantly, holding press conferences helps you to seize the initiative and manage the flow of information about what has happened.

These benefits depend upon the fact that you have prepared for the conference. You first need to decide how long you're going to let the conference run. Particularly if you are involved in an on-going incident, it is perfectly acceptable to explain at the outset of the conference that you can spare only forty-five minutes because you need to get back to dealing with the problem (I wouldn't suggest less than thirty minutes — it makes the conference of dubious value and would certainly antagonize the press).

With diagrams, models or any other means at your disposal begin the conference by introducing the others hosting the conference, and the roles that they are playing in coping with the situation. Then take your time in explaining exactly what has happened, how the situation has evolved, what has been or is being done about it, and the other organizations with whom you may be cooperating. Above all, if it's that kind of situation, express regret and concern for what has happened and always remember to put people before property if both are involved. Then throw the conference open for questions but be firm in taking one question at a time and make sure it has been answered to your full satisfaction before accepting the next one. Involve your colleagues in answering the questions, as appropriate.

Make sure that your public relations advisors have helped you to anticipate the likely areas of questioning and that the answers have been thought through. Don't get stuck on questions which you are not yet in a position to answer. Say you can't answer that question yet (but try to give a sensible reason) and move the questioning on by employing techniques like, 'but I can tell you that . . .'

When getting towards the end of the allotted time for

the conference, wrap it up by using a phrase like 'I've got time to take just one more question . . .'

It's often at the end of the conference that people make their biggest mistakes. Once the conference is at an end, make sure you and your colleagues have an escape route so that you are not pursued down corridors with people still asking questions. It's then that you are off your guard and might slip into saying something which could come back to haunt you. On the other hand, don't look as if you're trying to escape from the press conference. Simply use a different exit from that used by the press. They've had their opportunity to talk you: now it's time to get back to the business of dealing with the problem.

Carry on holding press conferences every day (twice a day if merited) until the episode is over.

Keep in control; be truthful, don't speculate, don't use jargon and don't apportion blame. If blame is to be apportioned it will be the job of the courts or an official enquiry.

In Dow Canada Inc, 'no comment' is recognized as an inept and totally unacceptable response. Somebody once said, 'freedom of the press is a right, freedom from the press is an illusion'. Dow Canada's Donald Stephenson says: 'Our people discovered that all the statistics in the world are seldom enough to sway public attitudes. Masses of data bore an audience. They cause people to turn off unless you simplify by combining the key facts with emotion, then orient your message so it shows a sincere appreciation of the people you are addressing.'

Dow Canada's corporate bywords are these:

1 *honesty* first, foremost and always

2 *empathy* and *compassion*

3 *openess, accessibility* and *candour*

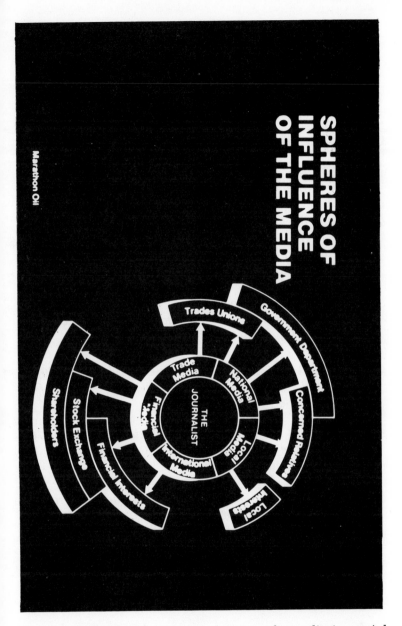

Figure 6.3: Getting the message across to the media is crucial because of its sphere of influence on other external groups.

4 *timeliness*

5 *proactive*, not simply reactive

Communicating in crisis

1 *Identify the media, with names, addresses and telephone numbers.*

2 *Prepare background information packs on each part of the organization considered to be at risk; keep them updated and located both at headquarters and the site of the installation at risk.*

3 *Establish a press room which can be used for press conferences and as a focal point where the media can collect the latest information.*

4 *Set up an emergency press centre to take incoming calls from the media. Man it twenty-four hours a day if necessary.*

5 *Ensure that the senior public relations representative is part of the crisis management team, located in the emergency control centre.*

6 *If possible, designate a quiet room adjacent to the emergency control centre in which to locate the crisis management team leader and the press release writer.*

7 *Prepare a contingency press release leaving gaps which can be quickly filled in when and if something goes wrong.*

8 *Issue new press releases as more known facts become available.*

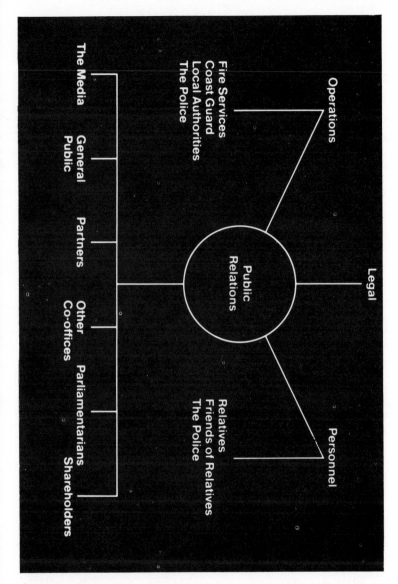

Figure 6.4: Communicating facts about what has gone wrong and what is being done to remedy the situation requires a managed flow of information, from a central source, both internal and external to the organization.

9 *Distribute press releases to other key players, both inside and outside the organization, before distributing them to the media.*

10 *Make sure the switchboard knows from whom to expect calls and to whom they should be routed, in the event of a crisis.*

11 *Announce the timing of press conferences as soon as possible to alleviate pressure from incoming media calls.*

12 *Prepare thoroughly for each press conference.*

13 *In all communication, be truthful, don't speculate, don't use jargon and don't apportion blame. Express regret and concern for what has happened. Always put people before property.*

Bibliography and references

Donald R Stephenson, 'Converting crises into cheers: deeds versus declarations', *International Public Relations Review*, August 1985.

R C Dilenschneider and Richard C Hyde, 'Crisis Communications: planning for the unplanned', *Business Horizons*, January-February 1985.

'How companies are learning to prepare for the worst', *Business Week*, 23 December 1985.

CHAPTER 7

Prevention is Better than Cure

This book has been about seizing the initiative; about anticipation and planning; about procedures, communications and training. Its underlying theme has been that prevention is always better than cure but, when faced with disaster, a proactive, thought-out approach can help to minimize the damage to your corporate reputation.

In this final chapter I want to emphasize the importance of not being lulled into a false sense of security, of not blindly believing your own public relations machine, confusing image with reality. An example of this fatal confusion of image with reality became apparent at the very inception of NASA's space shuttle programme, which led to the flight of the doomed space shuttle *Challenger*.

NASA officials, fearful that they could not otherwise obtain congressional funding, mounted an energetic public relations campaign that depicted the shuttle as all things to all people. The agency promised that the shuttle would lift scientific payloads into orbit, provide the Pentagon with access to the 'high ground' of space, and offer an efficient, economical means of launching communications satellites which could turn a profit into a bargain. As Timothy Ferris pointed out in his excellent article, 'The year the warning lights flashed on', the shuttle's promoters viewed the future through glasses as rosy as those worn by the Soviet engineers who employed nuclear power to steam-heat the suburbs of Gorky and Odessa.

Ferris pointed out that the real shuttle could no more

fly, at a profit, once a fortnight than it could speed Mr Spock to the stars.

Faced with spiralling costs and ever-lengthening delays, NASA cut back its training programme, cannibalized parts from other spacecraft and deferred the spending of half a billion dollars on safety. There was an increasingly wide gap between the facts and the shuttle's glowing public image. NASA officials increasingly chose to believe in the image, which, in turn, drifted ever further from reality. The odds of a fatal shuttle crash were variously estimated at one in a hundred to one in a hundred thousand; the *Challenger* mission, the programme's 25th, proved that these odds had been estimated too high.

The justification for NASA's trust in its flawed spacecraft was reduced to the fact that it hadn't blown up yet. As at Chernobyl, the accumulation of an impressive safety record in the past came to be taken as a guarantee that nothing could go wrong in the future.

'The argument that the same risk was flown before without failure is often accepted as an argument for the safety of accepting it again', noted Richard Feynman, the Nobel Prize-winning physicist who served on the presidential commission. But, Feynman added, 'when playing Russian roulette, the fact that the first shot got off safely is little comfort for the next'.

It was Feynman who cut through reams of bureaucracy on the O-ring question (which caused the space shuttle failure) by simply immersing a piece of O-ring material in a bucket of iced water during a break in the committee hearings and noting that it grew brittle. The trouble with NASA's belief in its own press clippings, Feynman said, was that nature had not read them. 'Reality must take precedence over public relations', he concluded, 'for nature cannot be fooled'.

Public outrage at the consequences of the mismanagement of industry — usually the result of greed, ignorance, complacency and want of care, coupled with the law's failure to provide an effective remedy — is mounting every day. And the prospect of a lessening in the numbers of corporate crises does not look promising.

Fires, explosions, toxic gas, radioactivity, and the dumping of oil, chemicals and industrial waste are contaminating more land, air, rivers, and sea, and killing and injuring more people than ever before. Moreover, the statistics show that the scale and frequency of those events increases year by year.

Late in 1986, 30 tons of agricultural chemicals were washed into the Rhine during a fire at the giant Sandoz plant in Basle, Switzerland. Ten days later the resulting 25-miles slick of toxic 'soup' was diluted in the North Sea. Like the Bhopal, Chernobyl, and *Challenger* tragedies before it, the Sandoz incident comes under the heading, 'accidental but avoidable'. Cruel fate took a hand, but shirked responsibilities and human failings gave it a flying start.

The Sandoz incident has focussed attention as never before on an industrial pollution problem that was there anyway, on the record of the Rhine-bank chemical firms in meeting their responsibilities, and on the will of governments to control them. Numerous relatively minor pollution accidents which have occurred since the Sandoz fire might have gone unnoticed were it not for the political spotlight that was turned on them. Such was the distrust that the authorities pledged to keep tabs on oxygen levels in the river to ensure that managements did not pump out waste slyly under cover of the central scandal. Ironically, however, three months after the Sandoz fire, the disaster seemed to have evaporated as an issue of international concern. Mostafa K Tolba, executive director of the UN Environment Programme, believes that this is typical of the catharsis and ultimate forgetfulness that has long accompanied such disasters. 'Perhaps it is a way of relieving anxieties about the dangers of modern technology', he says. 'If it were a process that elicited a coherent response to the dangers of toxic chemicals, all would be well. But there has been a tendency to let issues fade before any serious effort is made to prevent such disasters from recurring.'

Recently, he points out, there have been signs that things may be changing. For example, in response to the Bhopal tragedy, the United States Environmental Protection Agency introduced a programme to alert communities to toxic chemicals in their areas and to involve them in contingency plans. In the same way, Chernobyl has led to two international treaties on notification and assistance in case of nuclear accidents. EEC countries are now required to implement the *Seveso Directive* by identifying and controlling major industrial hazards.

Contingency plans, procedures for notification, chemical identification and early assistance are not costly measures. 'Beyond them', believes Mr Tolba, 'there is a need for national regulations, particularly in setting safety standards. If Sandoz and Union Carbide had been encouraged to play a more constructive role in contingency planning, perhaps their disasters would have been less catastrophic.

'In addition, statutory regulations require a national commitment to monitoring compliance with their standards. Progress is not simply a measure of mechanical competence. It includes an ability to formulate a coherent response to failure. It requires a package of international legislation that will organize procedures for notification and assistance in the case of chemical energy. And it should include a programme to alert local people to the chemicals with which they live and to help limit the dangers facing them.'

The attention paid to all forms of corporate crises, the increasing accountability to external groups for their actions, places organizations operating in risk areas firmly in the public spotlight.

Politicians are under pressure to tighten laws which govern safety standards and to provide harsher penalties for those who endanger life, pollute or defraud, as well as greater and speedier levels of compensation to those affected.

The continued inability of organizations, whatever their sphere of operations, to regulate their activities, so that crisis is minimized; a failure to check constantly that their deeds match up to their expectations and declarations; and lassitude over plans and preparations for the worst, so that crisis can be quickly contained, must inevitably lead to greater constraints being placed upon companies of all types.

The key to crisis management is crisis prevention, whether the vigilance and preparation is self-motivated or enforced by legislation. But if a fire does break out, comprehensive contingency planning can minimize the catastrophe; and a policy of open communication can minimize damage to corporate and individual reputations.

Crisis management summarized

Planning for crisis

1   *Develop a positive attitude towards crisis management.*

2   *Bring the organization's performance into line with public expectation.*

3   *Build credibility through a succession of responsible deeds.*

4   *Be prepared to act on the opportunities during a crisis.*

5   *Appoint a crisis management team.*

6   *Catalogue potential crisis situations.*

7 *Devise policies for their prevention.*

8 *Formulate strategies and tactics for dealing with each potential crisis.*

9 *Appoint crisis control and risk audit teams.*

10 *Identify who will be affected by any given crisis.*

11 *Devise effective communications channels for minimizing damage to the organization's reputation.*

12 *Seek outside expert advice when drawing up crisis contingency plans. Don't reinvent the wheel.*

13 *Put the plan in writing.*

14 *Test, test and test again.*

15 *Look at what specialized training programmes may be required to ensure you have a professional group of people around you.*

Planning for communications in crisis

1 *Be prepared to demonstrate human concern for what has happened.*

2 *Be prepared to seize early initiatives by rapidly establishing the company as the single authoritative source of information about what has gone wrong and what steps the organization is taking to remedy the situation.*

3 *Identify the media, with names, addresses and telephone numbers.*

4 *Identify other key external groups with whom communications would need to be maintained.*

5 *Prepare background information packs on each part of the organization considered to be at risk; keep them up-to-date and located both at headquarters and the site of the installation at risk.*

6 *Establish a press room which can be used for press conferences and as a focal point where the media can collect the latest information.*

7 *Develop a cascade call-out list for all those designated and trained to facilitate communications during a crisis.*

8 *Set up an emergency press centre to take incoming calls from the media. Man it twenty-four hours a day if necessary.*

9 *Ensure that there are sufficient personnel within the organization trained to help cope with incoming media calls, and calls from other external groups.*

10 *Ensure that the senior public relations representative is part of the crisis management team, located in the emergency control centre.*

11 *If possible, designate a quiet room adjacent to the emergency control centre in which to locate the crisis management team leader and the press release writer.*

12 *Prepare a contingency press release leaving gaps which can be quickly filled in when and if something goes wrong.*

13 *Make sure the switchboard knows who to expect calls*

from, and to whom they should be routed, in the event of a crisis:

Dealing with crisis

1 *Faced with disaster, consider the worst possible scenario — and act accordingly.*

2 *At the outset of a crisis, quickly establish a 'war room', or emergency control centre, and staff it with senior personnel trained to fulfill specific roles designed to contain and manage the crisis.*

3 *Trust the press office and keep it up-to-date with developments as well as steps being taken to control the situation.*

4 *Set up telephone hotlines to cope with the floods of additional incoming calls that will be received during a crisis. Have personnel trained to man the hotlines.*

5 *Know your audience and listen to their grievances. Ensure that you have a clear picture of their grievances against you. If possible, use research to verify your beliefs.*

6 *Get your opponents on your side by getting them involved in resolving the problem.*

7 *Add credibility to your cause by inviting objective, authoritative bodies to help end the crisis.*

8 *Always expect the unexpected. Be prepared to change plans as things never go accordingly to plan; and never underestimate the gravity of the situation.*

9 *Unorthodox methods of operation are often essential so the ability to bend the rules can prove vital.*

10 *Attach no stigma to employees who want to leave when a crisis occurs. Let them go. There are enough problems to cope with without having to look after less stable staff members.*

11 *Communicate the situation to head office, on a regular basis, without dramatizing it. Remember that media reports which head office is receiving tend to play up the most threatening aspects of the situation.*

12 *Be prepared to cope with an extended period under a high level of pressure and stress. So do not exceed normal levels of alcohol and cigarettes — reduce them if possible.*

13 *When the dust has settled, look to see what lessons you might be able to teach the rest of industry from your experience — and act accordingly.*

Communicating in crisis

1 *Start issuing background information about the organization as soon as possible after the onset of crisis, demonstrating your preparedness to communicate during the crisis — while providing valuable breathing space to prepare accurate press statements about what has gone wrong and what steps are being taken to remedy the situation.*

2 *When short on facts about what has, or is, going wrong, make your own news to fill the void until accurate information about the incident is available for dissemination.*

3 *Never fill the void with speculation or blatant untruths.*

4 *Issue new press releases as more known facts become*

available. Make sure others, to whom the press will be talking, also receive copies of the releases so that 'everyone sings off the same hymn sheet'.

5 *Announce the timing of press conferences as soon as possible to alleviate pressure from incoming calls. Prepare thoroughly for each press conference.*

6 *Remember the media do not work from nine-to-five. Particularly if a major catastrophe is involved, the company will be receiving calls from all around the world, from journalists operating in different time zones. Man the press office twenty-four hours a day, if necessary.*

7 *If wrongly accused of a misdemeanor, leave no stone unturned in proving the accusation to be false.*

8 *Develop a wide variety of information sources. Cultivate journalists and local opinion formers. Keep up-to-date on reports on local radio, television and the press.*

9 *Whenever possible, look for ways of using the media as part of your armoury for containing the effects of the crisis.*

10 *In communicating about crisis, avoid the use of jargon. Use language that shows you care about what has happened and which clearly demonstrates that you are trying to put matters right.*

11 *Ensure that the organization has a list of responsible deeds and actions behind it to support the credibility of statements and claims made during the crisis situation.*

Bibliography and references

Timothy Ferris, 'The Year the Warning Lights Flashed on', *LIFE*, January, 1987.

Mostafa K Tolba, 'Disastrous cycles of forgetfulness', *The Times*, 12 February, 1987.

Index